mY Generation

mY Generation

a real journey
of change and hope

josh james riebock

BakerBooks
a division of Baker Publishing Group
Grand Rapids, Michigan

© 2009 by Josh James Riebock

Published by Baker Books
a division of Baker Publishing Group
P.O. Box 6287, Grand Rapids, MI 49516-6287
www.bakerbooks.com

Printed in the United States of America

Library of Congress Cataloging-in-Publication Data
Riebock, Josh James, 1979–
    My generation : a real journey of change and hope / Josh James Riebock.
        p.   cm.
    Includes bibliographical references.
    ISBN 978-0-8010-7198-0 (pbk.)
    1. Church work with young adults. 2. Church work with youth. 3. Generation Y—Religious life. I. Title.
BV4446.R54 2009
259′.23—dc22   2009025225

09   10   11   12   13   14   15   7   6   5   4   3   2   1

In keeping with biblical principles of creation stewardship, Baker Publishing Group advocates the responsible use of our natural resources. As a member of the Green Press Initiative, our company uses recycled paper when possible. The text paper of this book is comprised of 30% post-consumer waste.

green
press
INITIATIVE

This is for us,
my generation,
a people I believe in and love.

Thank you . . .

Kristen.
You are beautiful in every way, and in every
way, you make me more beautiful.
I love you.

Mom. Dad.
I am so proud of you both and know you are of me.

Corbett, Quinn, Kraig, Kelly, and Grandma.
Ken, Becky, Ryan, Jason, and Brandon.
Because of you, I always have a home.

Chip.
You are my Morpheus. You gave me the red pill.

Eric Klein.
For talking me out of the rat poison time and
time again, and for believing when few did.

Micah, J. Burick, Henley, Baxter, Ben Grice, Alex M.,
Sagen, Davis, Justin Girdler, Sledge, Ralphy, Jon Peacock,
Governor Wisdom, and Matt Harrison Golley.
You are my best friends, my brothers and sister.

Master Kirchoff, Sam Mac, Joe Mac, Strom, Fowler,
Tommy Aagaard, Chris Flores, Nancy Whitworth,

A and T Paulson, The Reyna, Pat "Skulls" Illingworth, Danny Orr, Bill Orris, Matt and Kori Hockett, Tim Barg, Axel, Lane Wood, Nate Navarro, Selvaggio, "Wade," and Andrew Carpenter. What friends you are. What things you've given. What memories I have.

Baker Publishing Group. Jack. Chad Allen. Robert Hand. Matt Adams. Gateway. John Burke. Charles. Ted. GE Cov. FLI. WA. You've all offered me opportunities that I don't deserve and taught me things that cannot be measured.

The Mangan family and all those in my giving tree. You've done so many things I could never do, and done them all in faith.

Daniel Wallace, Sara Gruen, Rob Bell, Tim Burton, Donald Miller, and Christopher Nolan. You inspired me to be creative and honest. Thanks for giving us *Big Fish* (the book), *Water for Elephants*, *Velvet Elvis*, *Big Fish* (the movie), *Blue like Jazz*, and *The Dark Knight*.

And all others who have been and remain a part of me.

Contents

Contents

A Note from the Author

Thank you so much for opening this cover. Before you continue, I'd like to say something.

1. Yes, I've changed most of the names you are going to read about. I'm not completely sure why, but I felt like I should. So I did.
2. I wrote everything out as best as I could remember it. As I mention at a few points throughout this book, my memory is a finicky one, and I often can't remember things as well as I'd like. So with places, conversations, and events where I couldn't recall all the specifics, I recreated them as best I could according to the way I do remember them.

Prelude

Portrait of a Generation

You'd swear my friend David just walked out of the Vietnam War. His Rambo-like bandana keeps his wavy blond Afro from rising another three inches, and beer bottle caps line the front zipper of his faded military vest. I couldn't tell you what color eyes he has; I don't think I've ever seen them. Round mirror aviator shades conceal them nearly always. His lanky skeletal frame conjures images of a modern-day Ichabod Crane from *The Legend of Sleepy Hollow*, and much of his visible skin is covered in tattoos, which, I should mention, were done by David in his basement. For the most part, the tattoos are all one color, but full of creativity nonetheless. I think my favorite would have to be the one that spans eight knuckles and reads "COPS SUCK." David is Generation Y.

Years from now you may open a yearbook, and after you flip through all the outdated hairstyles and Spanish Club photos, you will eventually land upon a person who stood out in seemingly everything. When you do, you will be looking at the face of Katie. Katie is all-American—every guy wants her and every girl wants to be her. She is beautiful, athletic, and intelligent, but all the attention and accolades have not turned her into some sort of spoiled prima donna. On the contrary, she is sincere and caring, humble, and willing to walk alongside people as they struggle and learn. That's exactly why she is so good at her job as an elementary school teacher. Katie is Generation Y.

Around the office, he is well liked by fellow employees, and I'm not at all surprised. My friend Cyrus is a brilliant and skilled young office manager who knows how to positively motivate and encourage his coworkers. People like working for Cyrus and Cyrus likes working for the betterment of people, but not just around the office. When he's not working, he travels all over the world, offering himself and his skills to those suffering at the hands of deadly disease. Cyrus is Generation Y.

If ever you find yourself at an artistic-type coffeehouse near Chicago on a Saturday afternoon, you may run into Dan. He thinks deeply about life and questions everything, even the stuff that everyone tells him you aren't allowed to question. He refuses to consume ideas as truth until he has considered, examined, and tested them for himself. While sipping his coffee, he prefers to sit in a dim corner, listen to acoustic music, scribble thoughts in a journal, and remain within arm's length of a philosophy book. And though he doesn't know where his life is headed, he knows without a doubt that wherever it takes him, he will be raising questions every step of the way. Dan is Generation Y.

You know that girl walking down the street in the death metal shirt? That's my friend Sarah. She doesn't let anyone else define her. She is who she is and she isn't going to apologize for it anytime soon. Not only is she free about who she is, she also allows and draws that quality out of the people around her. Like a corkscrew, she unleashes the unique personalities and styles of others that would otherwise remain trapped forever. I guess you could say that as Sarah goes, a trail of creativity is left in her wake. Sarah is Generation Y. Millions of people scream for Jake. You may very well be one of them. He is in a band with a number one song, a Grammy nomination, and a tour that sells out venues globally. A talented musician, he never gave up on the dream that his guitar would take him around the world. But in spite of all the success, notoriety, and fame, he remains faithful to his wife, and in his humility, recognizes that he is the same person now as he was when he was strumming in his dorm room, with no audience but himself. Jake is Generation Y.

And then there's me.

As a kid, I lived with my family in a red brick house on President Street. It had a wooden front porch, blue shutters, and thirteen cats. My sisters and I took the time to painstakingly name every last one of them.[1] Five houses away, in a brown house with a circle driveway, lived a pretty little Dutch girl named Kristen. Today, all the cats are dead, and Kristen and I are married. Growing up, I loved sports and still do, though my heart is, and always has been, more passionate about art. You know: film, music, and theater. I suppose that's how I got into leadership in the first place, by playing Noah in my sixth grade class's production of *Noah and the Ark: The Musical.*

Since my days on that bright stage, I've had the opportunity to lead in a variety of ways, some of them vocational and others just a part of everyday life.

1979–Present: Brother

I have two full sisters. Corbett Ann is older than me, and Quinn Alexis is younger. They have the unique names.

15

1982–Present: Friend

This isn't just padding my résumé. To me, much of true friendship is leadership. It's pushing people to become who they want to become and can become. I think it's one of the purest forms of leadership, one that can't be understated, and one that, to some extent, we all hold. This means that in some ways, whether we like it or not and whether we accept it or not, we're all leaders.

July 1997–December 1997: Waiter at Bakers Square

Best pies in the world.

1997–2005: Basketball and Soccer Coach

June 1998: Housepainter

This lasted all of three weeks. I was convinced that if I stayed much longer, I'd go crazy, so I quit and moved to Mexico City for three months. I said I was going to take classes at the national university and further my higher education, but really, I was just chasing a cute blonde-haired girl from Maryland.

1999–2000: Janitor

One of the best jobs I've ever had. I'd show up after midnight, clean toilets, empty wastebaskets, mop floors, and listen to music. Sometimes I sang really loudly to Guns N' Roses while doing that Axl Rose snake slither dance and pantomiming that my mop was a microphone. I'm really thankful no one ever walked in on that, or at least if they did, that they never said anything.

1999–2003: Wilderness Guide

2002–2008: Pastor

I did this in two different churches, and a lot of people say I was quite "successful." I'm not really sure what they mean by that, and I'm even less sure that they're right. While some amazing things happened in the lives of people in both places, I think it was virtually always in spite of me rather than because of me.

2005–Present: Spouse

2007–Present: Speaker and Writer

This is what I do for a living now.

Everything there has involved Generation Y and taught me a great deal about both them and me, but there's a small twist to all this.

Do you remember that Hair Club for Men commercial in which the guy says, "I'm not only the president, but I'm also a client"? My situation is kind of like that. I do consider myself a leader of this generation, but I'm also a member of it. Actually, that's how I see myself first and foremost, as simply a member. I too am Generation Y.

Do you understand us yet? If not, welcome to the club. Most days, I don't either.

The truth is, it's hard to concretely define or understand any generation. Generational DNA materializes according to the way that millions of people collide with what is happening in the world around them, and there's nothing simple about that. Generations are complex, deep, and diverse, with endless nuances. No one can sum one up in a few sentences; certainly not me. But let me give you a snapshot of us, as a generation, for frame of reference sake, according to relevant research and my own experience.

Most date us as individuals born between the late '70s and the early '90s, give or take a few years.[2] So when it comes to music, we missed out on disco, but we were there for the end of hair bands and grunge, and the emergence of Britney Spears and hip-hop.

In the world of television, we don't know who shot J. R. on *Dallas*—so don't ask—but we know who shot Mr. Burns on *The Simpsons*. We are the people of *Seinfeld*, *Lost*, *Friends*, *The Office*, and the unfortunate genre of reality shows. For us, the golden age of *Saturday Night Live* is not the casts including Dan Aykroyd, Eddie Murphy, and Gilda Radner, but the casts including Chris Farley, Adam Sandler, Mike Myers, and Will Ferrell. When it comes to the silver screen, our *Star Wars* is called *The Matrix* or *Harry Potter* and our *Animal House* is called *Old School* or *Dumb and Dumber*. Our *Friday the 13th* is called *Saw* and our *Gone with the Wind* is *Good Will Hunting*. In the world of professional sports, you may call the greatest Muhammad Ali, Wayne Gretzky, or Hank Aaron, but according to us, Michael Jordan or Tiger Woods deserves that title.

We are the generation of tattoos, extreme sports, and Starbucks; the generation of video games, the Internet, cell phones, social networking, and iPods. We are the generation of authenticity, social justice, a new kind of church, racial diversity, professional flexibility, tightly knit communities, and overnight sensations. We are dreamers, hopers, innovators, idealists, peacemakers, and imaginaries.

We are Generation Y.[3]

We are great and we are many—at last count, over 70 million in the United States alone. We are brimming with potential waiting to be released, and we have the power to usher beautiful change into the world unlike any generation before us.

But we are also a broken generation.

Take my friend David, for example. While the self-tattooing Vietnam-esque renegade is immensely creative and free, he is also struggling mightily. Drugs have owned much of his life, and his belief that "Cops Suck" comes from a fat log of run-ins with the law that have landed him in juvenile detention centers and jail on multiple occasions. His mom paid him little attention growing up, and for most of his life he bounced around from one of her boyfriend's houses to the next. Today,

David isn't really sure if anyone wants him around, and in his most honest moments, he isn't sure if he wants to be around anymore either.

And Katie, the all-American elementary school teacher I mentioned before? Well, her life isn't perfect nor is she without her own scars. On a lonely night some years ago, she prematurely slept with a boyfriend, and her life has never been the same. She feels used and now carries an overwhelming, heavy weight of shame on her shoulders. Her beliefs and judgmental religious community tell her that God sees her differently now, and that is almost too much for her sweet heart to bear.

As for Cyrus, my caring and savvy manager friend, I only wish his own family offered him the same support and encouragement that he offers to so many. Cyrus recently told them that he has AIDS, a disease he contracted through a boyfriend years ago. The news not only devastated them, but it disgusted them as well. Now, pushed away by those he loves, Cyrus drowns his pain and rejection in busyness and work.

Dan, the contemplative guy you would find in the coffee shop, isn't sure he can contribute to the world. Since childhood, he's battled weight issues, and a deep root of insecurity resides in his soul, stemming from two decades of taunts and cold comments. The saddest part is that until he sees and believes for himself that, though he isn't perfect, he has a lot to offer, the world will go without the insights of his mind and heart.

And while Sarah may express herself freely on the surface, be assured, brokenness is all over her life. Her parents divorced when she was in grade school, and now her father rarely speaks to her. His wounding is so deep that he once locked himself in his bedroom, eating jars of peanut butter and bags of M&M's as a means to kill himself. Sarah's mom suffers from extreme depression and bipolar disorder and is on the verge of giving up on her daughter altogether. So for months at a time, Sarah lives with her brother on a ranch in Wyoming, where she knows no one and no one knows her.

The rock star Jake? Yeah, everyone loves him, except for the one person whom he wants most to be loved by: his wife. As he reached the pinnacle of success and opportunity, she came clean about her marital unfaithfulness. Needless to say, Jake was devastated. From there, things fell apart pretty quickly, ending their one-time electric romance in divorce. Jake's soft heart is now covered in a rough shell of bitterness, hate, and skepticism.

And me?

Well, I'll get into more of that in the pages to come, but yeah, I'm broken too. We all are.

In addition to the potential, creativity, and beauty that is us, we are also the generation of broken homes, the Columbine massacre, loneliness, immense performance pressure, sky-rocketing costs of living, 9/11, violence, the AIDS pandemic, suicide, religious jadedness, self-indulgence, and insecurity.

Like I said, my generation is hurting. My generation is wounded. We're broken. We are in deep need of a change, of restoration, and as that reality sinks in, I'm swept up, swept off in a fantasy, but one that doesn't feel too far from my everyday reality.

A World Painted Ash

I don't know how I got here, but I'm here.

I'm standing on the top of a building made of mirrors and glass. It's tall. So tall, that when I reach over the side I can touch the clouds. I spin, looking far in all directions, but my eyes see nothing. Not trees. Not houses. Not even colors. I see nothing but a gray desert, a world painted ash, and it spreads as far as I can see. Wait.

I hear something, something rising up from below. It's a peculiar noise, a low rumble, but I can't make out what it is. I listen again, intently this time. I lean out over the edge as far as I can without tumbling over the side, and as I do, the noise swells, growing louder and louder. My head begins to hurt. Whatever it is, I don't want to hear it anymore, so I step away. But I can't escape the sound. It fills my ears, spilling into my skull, down my throat, and into my stomach, and as it does, I come to recognize it.

It's the sound of voices, of people, of familiar people, of my people, of me. It's the sound of my generation.

Slowly, I return to the edge and with perfect clarity I hear the voices band together in a broken symphony, playing sorrowful notes and pained chords. I hear flutes of doubt and fading hope, strings that weep of loneliness, horns shouting shame, and the unpredictable chimes of division and fear. I hear all of it rising up from the ashy world, the entire symphony, and as it plays, it cries. It cries for color, for healing, and for restoration. It cries for something new, something meaningful, for something, or perhaps, for someone.

This sound climbing from my generation is a cry for change. Wait.

My feet begin to lift off the building: first my heels, followed by my arches, and I'm helpless against it. My toes glide off and I float aimlessly, pushed back and forth by the gusts of wind. I'm a feather, and as I flutter away, the gray desert and building of mirrors and glass grow tiny, and the broken symphony fades from my ears. I'm swept back to where I came from, and questions echo somewhere within my heart and mind.

21

What can I do? What can you do? What can we do to answer the broken symphony, the cry for change? What can we do to bring restoration to this generation?

A Real and, at Times, Imaginative Journey Ahead

I'm back now, and I know that both inside and outside of my fantasy, these are the critical questions, because the reality of the brokenness is not a mystery to most, but what to do about it is where the fog feels particularly thick. At times, it seems like these questions have no answers, or at least no good answers. I hear plenty of bad ones.

Every now and again someone claims to have discovered the antidote or to have cracked the code, but I'm convinced that those people are privately wondering, "What the heck are we doing?" or "I can't believe they bought it." And just so you don't throw me into that camp, I'll tell you up front, I don't have the answer either.

So if you're looking for a "how-to" manual, then you've got the wrong book. This is not a "how-to" manual and, be assured, there is nothing foolproof about it. Restoration doesn't work that way, and anyone who tells you differently is trying to sell you something. So in here you'll find no snappy acronyms that you can put on a card, keep in your pocket, and regurgitate to someone else, because this isn't a formula. This book is about my journey, because I may not have the definitive answer on how to change the world, but what I can do is tell you how God has brought change in me and in those around me. And I want to warn you up front that this has had very little to do with new methods, strategies, and models. In fact, it's really not been about that at all.

As I look back, I see that it's been about something much greater than that.

This restoration has come in the internal depths, not the external edge, by way of the heart and mind, not just the eyes and hands. It's not been through stacking and filing, but twisting and turning, and it's been through patient healing, not quick fixes. It's not been through the always explainable, but often something strangely supernatural, by way of transformation, not information. It's come by walking a daring ancient corridor, not a safe and progressive one, and it hasn't so much been done, as much as it has happened. But even when it's happened, it's never been fully completed. It still needs to happen, again and again.

And as I have traveled this spiraling trail, I've seen God weave his way into the wounds of this generation and create something beautiful out of them. I've seen it in the Davids and the Katies. I've experienced it with the Sarahs and the Dans. And thanks to others, I'm experiencing it in my own heart as well.

So no matter who you are and how you are involved in my generation—whether you are a friend, a volunteer, a pastor, a student, a janitor, or, like me, a member—I want to invite you to come with me on this journey. Through the pages that follow, I invite you to dig deep into your heart, deep into the heart of a generation, and deep into the heart of God. And I pray that as you do, you will be inspired, filled with hope, and stretched to your uttermost brink.

This is my very real and, at times, imaginative journey. I pray that it points you in the direction of yours, and that through it you too might be used to restore my broken generation.

Things That Don't Matter

Three Short Stories of Things We Often Care about, Even Though Jesus Doesn't

Short 1:
How I allowed my concern for reputation to get in the way of loving people, especially people that were frowned upon by religious types, and how Jesus never did that, how he was a proud friend of sinners, and how if we lived the same way, this world might look a lot different.

I was a youth pastor at a small church for a while after college. It had heavily traveled, cracked concrete steps leading to the front door, a small playground in the back for little kids, and a humble wooden pulpit with the raised emblem of a cross standing at the front of the sanctuary. It's a great church, and it was in my time there that I met Phil.

He was eighteen years old and gentle, with a full-toothed smile, but both his gentleness and smile were seen less and less in those days. A year earlier, Phil lost both of his parents in a car accident. Like an avalanche, that incident buried him under mounds of grief and anger. He numbed it the best way he knew how, mainly by abusing drugs and alcohol. At first it was recreational dabbling, one weekend a month or at the occasional party, but it grew in regularity and intensity to the point where, on multiple occasions, it nearly cost Phil his life. But that didn't stop him.

He continued to elevate his wildness in most areas of life, and that reality, combined with a healthy dose of gossip among the religious community, earned Phil a notorious reputation. I guess you could say that he became something of an urban legend. He was the guy that parents warned their kids about, the one that innocent daughters and reputable sons were supposed to stay away from, lest they end up pregnant or in jail. And that reputation followed him everywhere he went, including an area basketball game.

It was the third quarter, thousands of fans were screaming, and I was there.

Walking in front of the maroon-clad student section, I heard my name faintly over the raucous crowd. Turning to my right and looking up about ten rows, I spotted Phil. He yelled something in my direction, but I couldn't hear him over the noise and he knew it, so he tried again. This time, as he did, the gym went suddenly quiet, allowing me and everyone else to perfectly hear Phil scream, "Josh! I'm totally coming to f—ing church this week!"

Immediately, I flinched. A warm, fuzzy sensation came over me, and everything slowed down, eventually freezing altogether—transforming people into stone sculptures, locking mixed expressions onto faces, and suspending drops of sweat and buttery popcorn kernels just inches above the floor. Then a pair of feelings began to rise up in me, feelings that I knew well, feelings that I was quite familiar with and could easily define.

#1 Embarrassment

    Main Entry: em-bar-rass-ment

    Pronunciation: \im-ba-res-ment\

    Function: *noun*

    1: something that embarrasses <The incident with Phil was a major embarrassment for Josh—such an embarrassment that Josh wanted to dig a hole, hide in it, make the hole more roomy, live in it, and never come out.>

#2 Afraid

    Main Entry: afraid

    Pronunciation: \a-frad *Southern also* e-frad\

    Function: *adjective*

    1: filled with fear or apprehension <Josh was afraid of the whispering Christians in the crowd, afraid of what they would think if they saw him talking to Phil.>

That's exactly how I felt, and I really didn't know how to respond, how I should respond, how Christians would want me to respond, how my church with the cracked concrete steps would want me to respond, or even how Jesus would want me to respond. I didn't know any of that, and I didn't know how to figure it all out while standing in the now-petrified gymnasium.

The only thing I knew was how Phil needed me to respond. That part seemed pretty obvious.

Like anyone, he needed me to be excited to see him. He needed me to say hi. He needed me to embrace him. He needed me to look at him and treat him like he wasn't an urban legend. He needed me to reach back to him and love him, to proudly proclaim in front of everyone, including all religious observers, that we were friends. I knew what Phil needed, and yet, it was the hardest thing for me to do.

At the time, the whispering Christians and their words mattered a lot to me. I cared a lot about what they thought. In many ways, I equated how spiritual I was with my reputation among them, and that made their opinion one of the most important things in my life. That only made my decision that much harder, because I already knew what they thought of Phil. They were one of the reasons he was an urban legend to begin with. So while I didn't know how they would want me to respond, I knew how they wouldn't want me to respond. They wouldn't want me near Phil.

So I stood there for a few seconds that felt like years: seconds so long, I felt as if I were aging before everyone's eyes—balding, forming wrinkles, and beginning to walk with a cane before the fourth quarter even started. But I needed every last second to decide what I was going to do, to decide what really mattered to me, to decide who really mattered to me.

Time began again, returning to regular speed, and when it did, everyone was looking at me. They were waiting.

Glancing up one more time, I looked at Phil. I looked closely at his face, at his eyes, and noticed that he was excited to see me. And as I did, I suddenly couldn't imagine Jesus not being thrilled to see Phil. I couldn't imagine, under any circumstances, that in that moment, Phil wouldn't be the most important thing to Jesus, the only thing that mattered. That's when it all made sense. That's when I made my decision.

So I yelled back, "I can't wait to see you there, man! And hey, would you like to get dinner sometime this week?"

In that moment, I no longer cared about being associated with Phil. Or maybe a better way to put it would be—I started caring about being associated with Phil. I wanted to be associated with Phil. I wanted him and every person in that gym, including all the whispering Christians, to know that he was my friend and I was his, and that I was proud of that fact, not ashamed of it.

And with what felt like the world watching, Phil smiled that full-toothed smile, one that hadn't been seen in a long time.

Short 2:
How what is considered relationally normal (e.g., boundaries and pace) can, at times, only get in the way of bringing change, and how Jesus often ignored what is considered relationally normal because of that fact, and how someone was willing to do that for me.

It was a Thursday evening around five o'clock, and I was in the parking lot of T.G.I. Friday's. That's that restaurant with the candy-striped awning, the sesame jack chicken strips, and the wait staff that wears the pieces of flair. Justin pulled in a few seconds later in a small black car. But before that, it was a Wednesday and I was at a bar, and a church service.

It sounds confusing, but it's not. It was a church service being held in a bar. That's where Justin and I met.

He's a filmmaker and has cool tattoos, so I was drawn to him pretty quickly, even if it was for superficial reasons. We hit it off, and after a brief conversation, decided to get together the following week, but that stirred all kinds of anxiety in me.

I'm not an overly social person to begin with, but I find the maiden voyage of hanging out with someone, anyone, borderline insufferable. The chances of me feeling and acting both distant and awkward are very good. To avoid the slightest dash of silence, I usually talk too much, often rambling about topics of no particular significance, and I can carry on that way for months.

That's part of why it takes me so long to make lasting friendships, because I resist intimacy like the plague. I distance myself. I push people away. I keep things impersonal, which, sadly, is the way I like it.

On the Monday following the church service, my phone rang.

"Josh?"

"Yeah," I said.

"Hey man, it's Justin."

"Oh, hey, bro." (I always call people *bro* when I'm uncomfortable.)

"What's going on? What are you doing?" he asked.

"Nothing much, bro" (see, I did it again right there), "what about you?"

"Not too much. I was just calling to see if you could hang out sometime this week?"

My chest tightened immediately. I guess I was hoping that he was merely being polite, saying that we would get together, but obviously he wasn't. Obviously, he meant it. Wanting our time together to be as nonthreatening as possible, I said, "Yeah. That'd be great. You want to grab a beer or something?"

That seemed safe enough. Lots of people. Plenty of noise. We could even sit on stools facing a wall instead of each other. What could possibly be safer than that? It seemed great, but Justin extinguished that idea.

"No, let's not do that. I'll tell you what, Josh. Don't worry about it. I'll take care of everything. Does Thursday, like around five, work for you?"

"Uh, yeah, bro," I said.

"Okay, well let's plan on Thursday at around five o'clock. You just meet me at the T.G.I. Friday's parking lot and I'll take care of the rest. . . . And Josh," Justin continued, "make sure you wear a rugged pair of shoes and a pair of shorts that you don't mind getting dirty."

I hung up the phone, reflected on one of the strangest conversations I'd ever had, and pretty much became a wreck.

What have I gotten myself into? Why does this weirdo want me to wear rugged shoes? Where the heck is he taking me? Maybe I'm going to be hunted for sport.

Oh God! It's like that movie Deliverance! *I think I hear that eerie banjo music now . . .*

Maybe his name isn't even Justin . . .

Yeah, I was a wreck. Confused. Curious. A little freaked out. Paranoid. Bearing a deep sense of regret that I'd answered my phone at all. A wreck. And I was that way for the next few days, but I still went, and that's how I ended up in the T.G.I. Friday's parking lot on that Thursday.

I stood next to my car, shifting my weight back and forth, and biting my nails practically down to the bone. Then Justin pulled into the parking lot. I opened the passenger-side door of his small black car, sat down, fastened my seat belt, and he began driving.

"So, where are we going?" I asked.

"You'll see," Justin said with a sly smile.

"Okay."

"This is really killing you, isn't it? Ha, that's great."

Eventually, we moved out onto a stretch of scenic highway and shortly after, Justin pulled into a lot at the base of a range of rocky cliffs, overlooking a lake.

"We're here," he said. "Come on."

He shut off the engine and got out of the car. I went with him as we walked toward a small hiking trail. Over the next fifteen minutes or so, we stepped up the side of the cliff, over stones and through the trees, finally settling at a lookout point with miles of visibility in either direction.

"I figured that I could have a beer with anyone," Justin said between heavy breaths. "But, and I hope this isn't weird, I really want to get to know you, to talk to you about deeper stuff, to hear what's really going on in your heart. I guess I really want to be friends, and I think this is a great place to do that."

I didn't know what to say. I was caught off guard, and apprehensive too, and yet, I was incredibly moved. I couldn't think of another time in my life when anyone had done that for me, when I mattered more to someone than what was considered normal, when someone was willing to ignore what I was comfortable with, in order to really love me. It was one of the most loving things anyone's ever done for me.

I guess you could say that what Justin did for me reminded me of what Jesus did for so many others—he refused to let expectations and what was considered normal get in the way of love.

"Thanks a lot, man. I'd really like that," I said.

I won't soon forget the hours that Justin and I spent on that cliff, talking about our wives, our childhoods, and God. Today, Justin is so much more than an acquaintance to me; he's a great friend, a friend of depth and intimacy, and that occasion started it all.

Short 3:
How when bringing restoration, I always wanted to see the results of my efforts, how I wanted people to change quickly and obviously (probably just so I could feel better about myself), and how maybe God doesn't; how maybe God is asking me to love people and leave the results to him.

Inhale.

> *Bright lime fire is leaking from the walls again, and that girl with the gills keeps waving at me. Stop waving at me!*

Why won't she just sit down on the nice marshmallow chair in front of her? It's soft and tasty, and it can see so well with its giant blinking eye.

Monocles, monocles, so many monocles.

Exxxhaaallllllllllle.

My mouth is dry, and I've got the munchies, but it feels good. I'm smoking weed. Again.

Ben is one of the most uplifting people in my life, one of my biggest purple balloons. He has a way of timing his emails, hugs, phone calls, face-to-face conversations, and text messages, and each time he offers one of these, I'm left believing that I can take on the world and win. Oh, and he used to smoke a whole lot of pot.

With his buddies, Ben would sit in a poorly lit basement somewhere and smoke. So later in the evening, when we hung out, he stunk like he just came from a Dave Matthews concert. We still had a good time when we were together (a great time, actually) and we talked about everything—dreams, music, his family, and even his struggle with pot—and we talked about it honestly. So I knew that he was a pretty big fan of pot, and he knew that I wasn't, but our disagreements didn't get in the way of our friendship.

We agreed to disagree. But I still wanted his lifestyle to change. I wanted him to change.

I wanted more than for Ben to stop smoking weed all the time. I wanted all the hurt from his family life to heal, his involvement in pornography to end, his heavy drinking to become moderate, and his lack of desire to have a relationship with Jesus to become a heavy, flaming, torrential hunger. I wanted Ben to change, and I wanted it to happen now, and I wanted to be the one to do it. One windy night, so windy that plastic bags were blowing through people's yards, wheeling and dragging as ghosts through a cemetery, I thought it was all going to happen.

We were at Ben's house watching a movie, one that I'd already seen twenty times. He was lying on the couch, and I was in the recliner.

"So, Josh, tell me more about this Jesus stuff," he said, seemingly out of nowhere.

"Really?" I said, plenty surprised. "Okay, I'd love to."

So we talked, and as the questions and conversation flowed, I began to form in my mind a Hollywood picture of how that night would end.

Ben begins to feel something inside, something he wants but doesn't recognize. It's God moving, inviting, and touching him. His eyes begin to sparkle, but tears aren't the cause. A Spirit aliveness is.

He rubs the back of his neck and says he wants this Jesus. He breaks down, out of joy. He wants to walk with the One that has loved him since time began. He wants to grow, to change. And he will.

His life is changing and other lives will change through him. Many. How many? I don't know. But mine will be one, I'm sure of it. It begins tonight. Tonight, so very bright.

Roll credits.

I envisioned all the things that I wanted, all the results that I was after, to finally be realized in one dramatic, cinematic scene. But none of it happened. In reality, as the credits rolled on that conversation, his climactic response was something like, "That's cool."

Not so Hollywood, is it? No, it's not. But a lot of the best stories in life aren't very Hollywood.

Often, the best stories aren't when someone pulls one 180-degree turn, but when someone pulls 180 one-degree turns: the stories when someone experiences a slow and, at times, indistinguishable evolution; the stories where a million tiny steps produce something so brilliant; the stories where perseverance and struggle go hand in hand. But I tend to forget how great those stories can be, and I forgot with Ben.

That windy night, his life didn't visibly, quickly change, and it didn't change the next night, or the night after that, or the night after that—and it all started to get to me.

Sometimes, after we were together, I found myself mired in a depressed state. I would drive home and listen to the only music that spoke my present emotional language: something like Nirvana, Counting Crows, or whatever else was sorrowfully good. I'd ask God and myself what I was doing wrong and wonder why I wasn't getting results. I even thought seriously about giving up on Ben altogether, just throwing in the towel and walking away. But I didn't.

I'm not exactly sure why.

All I can tell you is I slowly came to believe that just because Ben isn't changing in the way I want him to, that doesn't mean he isn't changing. I came to believe that just because I can't always see restoration, that doesn't mean restoration isn't happening. I came to believe growth, change, and healing can't necessarily be boxed, always quantified, or falsely accelerated. I came to believe that just because Ben wasn't sure about "all this Jesus stuff," that didn't mean Jesus wasn't sure about him, and what he's doing with him. And I also came to believe that maybe Jesus isn't asking me to get the quick, obvious, sexy, Hollywood results I'm often after—maybe he's just asking me to love Ben, and leave both the results, and what they look like, to him.

So I'm trying.

It's been years since those days, but Ben and I are still great friends, and he's still one of the most uplifting people in my life, one of my biggest purple balloons. He's grown a great deal and left a lot of his former vices behind, but he still isn't so sure about "all this Jesus stuff." Since I'm not the author of his story, I don't know how this is all going to end, but I can tell you that as long as the Author allows, I'm going to play my part in what is being written. I'm going to love my friend as best I can, with or without results.

The Greatest Show on Earth

Inviting Others into Change

I went to a tent revival once. My mom took my sisters and me.

It was a humid and suffocating summer, and my family was in northern Wisconsin. We vacationed there often when I was a kid, and I really liked it. During the day I could catch frogs and explore the woods, and at night I could see deer cross the road. On most weekends, we'd go into the local town to peruse flea markets and eat at The Colonial House, an old-fashioned ice cream parlor that boasted a player piano. My favorite song selection was *The Entertainer*. It was a great town, and it was there, one cloudy afternoon, that the band of religious nomads arrived and for an entire week, they set up in a field next to the grocery store. Everyone was buzzing. It was like the circus had come to town, THE GREATEST SHOW ON EARTH, and I guess in some ways, it had.

Along with a mass of eager people, we showed up on Friday night and poured into the blue-and-yellow-striped tent. It was high and pointed at both the center and corners, soaring like a canvas castle, and as we walked through the front flap, music blared, shouting and reeling us in. The crowd clapped in unison and swayed side to side; some people were dancing. The stage was big, but rudimentary: nothing more than a bunch of wood slabs dropped on top of faded cinder blocks. A man in a flashy suit was standing on stage, grinning and waving his hands, but in a way that felt unnatural, almost like he was trying to be something he wasn't. Still, I was curious about him and the rest of the festivities, but before I got a chance to see more, a young woman who smelled like sweet green apples took me softly by the hand and led me off. As I walked away, my mom gave me a reassuring wink and waved to me.

The young woman took me out another door along the side of the tent and into a smaller tent that, from the outside, seemed not nearly as special. The colors were faded and dulled and inside it was much quieter.

Stepping in, I saw only kids, young boys and girls that no doubt had come along with their families too. They sat on wooden benches and in the grass. There was no stage, only a small card table, on top of which sat a number of objects covered by a pink blanket. I remember thinking, *I wish I was still in the other tent.* The young woman took me into an aisle about five rows from the front, let go of my hand, and I sat down amongst the other kids.

A few seconds later, the show started.

A different young woman, this one with a floral-patterned dress and the kind of face that you could trust, walked out in front. She looked back and forth over the crowd, offered an energetic welcome, and then began preaching. At seven, I knew what preaching was.

My family went to church on most Sundays, though rarely the same one. Most of the time, we hopped around from one to another—Presbyterian, Episcopal, Bible Church, megachurch, small community church with hardly anyone there, traditional with hymns, contemporary with guitar and drums, formal, casual—always finding a reason to try something different. "I don't agree with their theology," my mom would say. "The pastor wasn't very engaging." "It's too old fashioned." "The service starts too early," my dad would say. "The service gets out too late," my dad would also say. "It just didn't feel right." There was always a reason. But I spent enough time in church that I was aware of when a sermon was coming. I had seen it and listened to pastors do it before, but never with this enticing of a hook.

"Someone here tonight," the woman with the floral-patterened dress said, "has an ailment. An illness. The Lord is telling me that someone here is sick."

Her voice quivered. She closed her eyes, like she was visualizing the answer that she was searching for.

"Yes! Someone here tonight has a stomachache! Whoever you are, your stomach is hurting! It hurts badly, but God wants to heal you!"

Her voice grew louder and she spoke with more fervor.

"Who is it? Who here has a stomachache?"

It was silent, uncomfortably silent. Even at seven, I knew what an uncomfortable silence felt like, and this was it.

"If you come forward . . ." she said, turning her back and walking towards the table with the pink blanket, her floral-patterened dress whirling, "if you are willing to come forward and be part of a miracle, you will have your choice of any toy you want!!"

As she finished her sentence, she yanked the pink blanket off the table like a magician performing a trick would, and all of our innocent eyes were met with piles and rows of un-opened action figures and dolls. They were shiny and perfect in every way, and I wanted them.

"Well?" she asked. "Who wants to be healed by God? Who needs God to touch their stomach tonight? Who wants to be a part of a miracle?"

Immediately, I shot my hand up into the air. My stomach didn't hurt. I didn't want to be healed. I certainly didn't want to be a part of a miracle. I wanted one of those toys.

"Praise Jesus!"

She shouted, and as she ran towards me all the other adults lining the perimeter of the tent began applauding, cheering, and waiving their arms back and forth. Taking my hand, she walked me to the front of the tent, but my eyes never moved from the table of toys.

"Young man, what is your name?"

"Josh," I said.

"Josh, your stomach hurts doesn't it."

It was more of a statement than a question, so I went along with it, nodding my head.

"Well, Josh, Jesus is going to heal you tonight! He is going to heal you, and all you have to do to receive this blessed healing is speak in tongues. Have you ever spoken in tongues?"

I shook my head no.

"Well, Josh, it's really simple. You just open your mouth and let noise come out, and if you trust in the Spirit, you will speak in tongues and God will heal you! Come on! Just open your mouth."

She closed her eyes again and lifted her hands towards the top of the tent, like a trapeze artist, trying to grab onto something. All the other kids were staring at me. I opened my mouth and awkwardly began to make noise.

"Blah. Blee. Blay. Bloo. Blahhhhhhh." I said, and as I did, the young woman placed her hand on my stomach and began to shout.

"PRAISE JESUS! PRAISE JESUS! You see! You see! He's speaking the Lord's language! He's speaking in tongues and he's being healed! Keep going, son! Keep going!"

Everyone started cheering, so I gave the crowd more of what they wanted.

"Blah-da-ho-ay! Blah-da-ho-ay! Blah-da-ho-ay!!"

"Hallelujah!" she said, along with some other things that I didn't understand. "Hallelujah!"

It's strange how perceptive and intuitive we are as kids. Even at seven years old, I knew it was a scam. I knew I wasn't speaking in tongues. I knew that she knew I wasn't speaking in tongues, but I also knew that she wanted everyone to think that I was. I knew that what I was doing had nothing to do with God. And somehow, I knew that I wasn't going to get a toy either, which I didn't. Apparently the toy table was nothing more than an attempt to lure me into a "miracle."

But looking back, that night wasn't, for me, just about leaving without a toy.

That night was, for me, the genesis of my heartless and hollow religion, of a façade, one that I lived for years. It was the beginning of my pharisaical life, of acting the part of what a Christian man was supposed to be (i.e., church attendee, Bible reader, Bible memorizer, public prayer volunteer, doer of the right things, hider of it when I didn't, talker of Scripture) but never really becoming a man after Christ. That night ignited for me a belief that God wasn't really who I hoped he was, a belief that he was more about illusions and cheap parlor tricks, like the Wizard presiding over Oz, than making people and things new. It was the beginning of my jadedness and cynicism, the beginning of a long struggle to trust both God and anyone claiming the name of Jesus.

It was the beginning of a struggle that many of us share, a struggle that Andy shared twenty years later, when we were introduced.

A Familiar Sort of Renaissance Cowboy

Andy is a really good friend, and the best way I can describe him is—Renaissance man. He's a:
Poet.
Athlete.
Musician.
Maker of good gifts.
Film lover. Filmmaker.
Philosopher.
Writer.
Romantic.
And he's a cowboy too.
He doesn't wear spurs or chaps. He doesn't ride a horse or carry a six-shooter. But to me, he's a cowboy nonetheless.
Giddy-up!
I had just moved to Austin from Chicago, and he was a film student at the University of Texas, when we met through a mutual friend. Smelling of chewing tobacco and sporting genuine boots, he used words like "fixin'," "reckon," and "y'all," and his faded and tight-fitting Wranglers left not nearly enough to the imagination. It's fair to say that meeting Andy was a little bit of a culture shock for me, but still, I liked him; plus there was something about him that was very familiar, so following our initial conversation I extended an invitation to barbeque the next week and he agreed.
A few days later, we met at Rudy's, my favorite restaurant/gas station in the world, and over jalapeno sausage and sweet tea I heard his story.

He was born in northern Texas, into a great Christian family that attended a small conservative church, so he grew up a bit sheltered, and developed a strong familiarity with Scripture at a young age. As he grew older he did the right thing on most occasions, and kept himself from wandering too far off the beaten moral path, but as I listened to him describe it all, something seemed to be missing.

"So I guess you'd consider yourself a Christian?" I asked. "A follower of Jesus? Or whatever other label you want to put on it?"

"Yea," Andy said, "I would."

"But . . ."

"What do you mean?" he asked.

"There's got to be more to it than that, Andy. Come on."

"Well, that's just it. There is no more to it. I'm a Christian. It's there, and there's nothing more to say about it."

"Okay," I said.

Andy's faith was far from passionate or alive. It was closer to jaded, indifferent, and decaying. There was a cynical nature to it, and that didn't offend me; I was just curious as to why. So after that first lunch and a horrible bout of indigestion, we decided to meet at Rudy's again the next week. That lunch turned into another, and another, and another and every week, Andy told me more of his story. Then, on a bright spring afternoon, he shared one of the moments that had shaped him most.

"Josh, when I was in high school, I knew this amazing guy that worked at our church. Everyone loved him, you know? I loved him too. He was one of those guys that I believed in and wanted to be like. A lot of the reason that I believed in God was because of him."

I had a sick feeling in my gut about where his story was heading and I hoped that I was wrong, but Andy's body language told me that I was right. His voice grew tense as he dug his elbows into the red-and-white checkered tablecloth.

"Well, one day he told everyone that he was leaving our church, 'in view of calling.' I didn't even know what that meant. 'In view of calling'? All I knew was that this guy that meant so much to me, this guy that I respected, this guy that loved God was leaving, and he did. He left . . ."

"I'm sorry, Andy."

"And then a few months later, I found out why he really left. He got fired for having sex with some girl in our youth group. Now what does that say about Christians? What does that say about God?"

"I don't know," I replied, sighing. "Nothing good."

"Yeah," Andy said, leaning back into his metal folding chair, "nothing good."

From that point in his life on, Christianity, for Andy, was nothing more than an act, a game that people played with their words and public lives, but one that never impacted their souls. Christians were phonies and actors, PEOPLEWHOCAN'TBETRUSTED. And God, well he became a giant question mark, a distant impostor that didn't really change people and heal hearts, a being who wasn't all everyone said he was, and not nearly who Andy hoped for or needed him to be.

Andy, like so many of us, was skeptical towards both God and Christians, and he'd grown weary of giving either another chance.

Two O'clock in the Garden of Eden

At two o'clock in the Garden of Eden, as the afternoon sun shone like a midday lantern, brilliantly, but not too hot, I climbed a tree and watched Beautiful Eve and Glorious God.

44

"Glorious God, are you what I hope you are?" Beautiful Eve asked.

"Well, I guess that kind of depends, Beautiful Eve. What do you hope that I am?"

"I knew you were going to say that."

Beautiful Eve paused for a moment, and then sat down on a log. I shifted my weight from one tree branch to another.

"Well, I guess I hope that you can do anything—including anything in me. I hope that you're always going to be close to me and never far away, and that you care about every single part of my life, not just some of it. I hope that you always know what's best for me, and that you'll always do what's best for me, even if I don't see how it's possibly what's best. And I hope that you love me more than I could ever understand, more than my mind could ever grasp, and that you like walking with me through this incredible world that you made."

"Is that all?" Glorious God asked.

"No, it's not. There's a lot more, but that's a good start," Beautiful Eve said.

There was a long pause, and neither of them said a word. Glorious God sat down next to Beautiful Eve.

"Beautiful Eve, are you waiting for me to tell you that I'm all those things that you hope for?"

"Well, to be honest, yeah, I guess I kind of am."

"I'm not going to tell you that, Beautiful Eve," Glorious God said gently.

"What?" Beautiful Eve asked, with a surprised tone and a stunned look. "Are you telling me that you aren't those things? That I can't trust you?"

"No. I'm not saying that. Not at all," Glorious God said, taking her hand in his. "I'm saying that I'm not here to try to convince you. I'm saying that I bring you into this world, into my world, so that you can seek me and know me for yourself.

I'm saying that I invite you to knock, to explore, and to taste all of me. I'm saying that I love you enough to let you find out for yourself if I'm what you're really hoping for. And if you do that, Beautiful Eve, you'll get your answer."

Sitting amongst the branches and leaves, I watched as Beautiful Eve looked at Glorious God and smiled. Beautiful Eve knew, just like I did, how deeply loving of an invitation that truly is. They stood up and walked away, talking and adventuring together through the Garden of Eden, and as they did, I leaned my head against the trunk of the tree, and began thinking.

I thought about how our world often only pushes people out, about how rare it is to be invited into someone else's life, and about how I often feel like the only people that invite me into their lives are those on television—some late night talk show host or weatherman. I thought about that feeling I sometimes get that I don't know some of my closest friends from Adam, anything about them, what they're thinking, what they like or why they like it—that feeling that they won't let me in.

A brown bird with white spots landed in the tree and sat by me. As it stood on the branch, it changed colors, becoming orange, with wings freckled blue and green. I looked at it. Then it flew away, landing near the creek. As it drank, I continued thinking.

I thought about how pretty it was, and how ugly Christianity often is.

Then I thought about the litany of stories detailing pastors bilking innocent people out of money, abusing kids, and having affairs. They smack us every day. I thought about how heartless Christianity often seems. I thought about how hard it is to get Christians involved in or excited about loving others, but how easy it is to get Christians involved in and excited about political agendas. I thought about how passionate Christians are about being right and how apathetic Christians are towards those in need. I thought about how my generation doesn't want that, how nauseating it is to us, how we don't want to become that. I thought about how jaded, cynical, and mistrusting my generation is towards God and Christians, how it's so hard not to be, and about how I, in many ways, feel the same way. I thought about how many of us, in my generation, are asking that same question of Glorious God, "Are you really what I hope for?"

And then I had an epiphany, an abrupt and mystical bolt to the head. I realized something.

I realized that, maybe, the greatest thing I can do for someone is not try to convince them that I can be trusted or that Glorious God is who they hope for, but maybe the greatest thing I can do for someone is invite them into my life to see Glorious God in me and let them decide those things for themselves. I realized that, maybe, the greatest thing I can offer someone is what Glorious God offered to Beautiful Eve, and what He offers to me—an invitation in.

And then I couldn't help but think about my friend Chip, about how he offered me this very thing, and about how it changed me, and my relationship with Glorious God, forever.

Chip, Up Close and Personal

Chip is a big fan of soccer and, tragically, the Detroit Lions.

He's fairly unassuming in his appearance, and idiosyncratic in personality, and his voice gets really high pitched and his face turns dark red when he laughs. But his heart, and the way it reflects what God can do in someone's life, is something to behold.

He came on staff at my school when I was seventeen, and though at the time my body was ten years older than that little boy from the tent revival, my heart hadn't aged at all. I was still that unbelieving, untrusting kid, the one who went through the motions of God and the one who thought that's what it meant to follow Jesus. I was still convinced that God and Christians were nothing more than a show, and so I acted the part, but none of it was real.

Anyway, almost immediately Chip reached out to me, not by sitting me down and telling me all the reasons that I needed God or attempting to convince me that he was different than the other Christians that I didn't trust. Instead, he did something that no one had ever done for me before.

Simply put, he invited me to know him.

He introduced me to his fiancée, Ingrid, and invited my friends and me over to his home. He told me about his parents, his upbringing, and his story of coming to know God, as well as his continuing journey to know him. He told me about his dreams, his ideas, and passions. He invited me to ask him questions, even personal questions. Through our time together, I saw what Chip wanted out of life. As he brought me in more and more, I trusted him more and more because I saw, for myself, that I could, and as I did, I experienced more of God through him. In Chip, faith suddenly became more than just a word, a Bible verse, or an idea. It became a real way of life. As I watched him interact with his family and friends, I saw a man of character, a man who loved people, someone who had been changed by something bigger than himself.

God used that relationship, over the course of a few years, to weaken my cynical nature, and as it weakened I not only opened my life more to Chip, a friend I now trusted, but more importantly, I slowly opened it to God.

It sounds funny, I guess, but the God I saw in Chip's life wasn't so much different, it's just that Chip actually let me see the God in his life, while everyone else just told me about him. Chip invited me in to see God and decide for myself if I wanted him, and when I was given that chance, I did.

So I started seeking him for myself.

Instead of sitting by and waiting for God to prove himself to me, to prove that my assumptions about him were wrong, I began to walk alongside him. I began to take small tastes of him, and when I did I found him to be nothing like the Wizard of Oz. He didn't want to hide or keep himself from me. He was willing to let me in, willing to let me know him. He was real. He was the kind of God that could heal me, and make me into the man that I desperately wanted to be. I found that God loved me deeply and cared about every single corner, hurt, doubt, and moment of my life.

He was everything that I hoped he was, and more.

Finally, after years of skeptical resistance, after years of living the Christian life and never knowing Christ, I invited God into my world, to know me, and I began to fall in love with him. Today, I'm still falling in love with him, and I trace a great deal of that love back to Chip. His willingness to invite me into his life was one of the greatest, and remains one of the greatest, things I've ever been offered. But what made my experience in Chip's world so profound was not simply that he invited me in, but what I found when I entered.

The Fine Print

It's late and I'm tired. Click.

I'm watching bad TV again. There's absolutely nothing good on. Reruns I've seen a dozen times. Hockey. C-movies. Two people selling puffy, Christmas sweaters. Click.

Late night TV is never good; that's why it's on late. But I'm watching anyway. Click.

I'm sure it'll get better. I'll find something decent. It can't stay this bad, right? Well, maybe it can. It has before. Click.

Recently, I saw an infomercial for a weight loss pill and like most, it promised that I could drop at least ten pounds in two weeks. Though I don't really need to lose ten pounds, for some reason I got excited, and I stayed excited until a chunk of fine print appeared on the bottom of the screen that only an Air Force pilot could read. It said, "This pill may cause headaches, high blood pressure, diarrhea, loss of feeling on the right side of your body, impotence, and possibly even death." At least I think that's what it said. As I mentioned, it was really small.

After I read that, my excitement all but died.

I watched for a little while longer and, for some reason, began thinking about this idea of inviting people into our lives. I thought about doing for others what Chip did for me, and I got excited, considering all the ways that lives could be changed just as mine was. But then I realized that this idea is a lot like that infomercial. It sounds great. It's exciting. But it also comes with fine print.

It says, "Inviting people into my world means that whomever I open my life to will see what is really going on in my life and heart." And just like it did with that infomercial, this fine print makes me think twice, and the truth is, it probably should. It should make all of us think twice, because the power of inviting people into our lives lies not only in inviting them in but also in what they find when they enter. And just so there's no confusion, I'm not talking about being perfect.

Pushing for a works-oriented, heavy-handed moral system that we must adhere to is not God's agenda or my own. I'm talking about living something that is imperfect, but real. I'm talking about being a person of love and becoming a person of character. I'm talking about loving God deeply, growing to love him more and more, and allowing him to love back. I'm talking about surrender, about making our lives available to God. I'm talking about genuine faith, walking with God daily and being changed.

I once heard someone say, "In order to be a part of the revolution, one must be a part of the evolution." I liked that a lot, and it made sense to me. We must always be changing, evolving, and becoming the people God created us to be in order to lead the revolution of others becoming who God created them to be. But this is a place so few are willing to go. This is a place I don't often want to go.

When it comes to the idea of change, I get much more jazzed about *bringing* it than *being* it. Watching someone else become a butterfly, after years of living as a caterpillar, is a spectacular thing, but when it's you becoming the butterfly you realize how painful a process it can be to leave that caterpillar life behind. Bringing change is thrilling. It makes great conversation. And best of all, it happens outside of my skeleton. Being changed is scary and it hurts. It's sometimes humiliating and often involves failure and discovering things about myself that I'd just as soon not discover. And worst of all, it's internal. But it's in that place of being changed, of putting myself in God's hands, of inviting him to work on who I am, of letting him teach me and discipline me, where my role in restoring lives originates and where it must always remain. So if I'm not up for that, if we're not up for that, for putting and leaving our lives in God's hands to be shaped and molded, we can invite others into our lives all we want, but it won't bring the kind of restoration God longs to bring. But for those who are willing, or want to be willing, to be continually transformed, perhaps the most powerful thing we can do for skeptical people, for my skeptical generation, is simply invite others in to see it.

Which takes me back to my relationship with Andy.

Jesus Cowboy

Andy didn't need someone who would try to convince him about God and Christians. He didn't need another person who wanted to get to know him. He needed someone who would invite him in and give him the space to decide for himself. He needed someone who was willing to be known. He needed someone who was willing to let him see the life-altering power of God, someone willing to show him God. Andy needed an invitation into my life, and I knew it. But that was a terrifying prospect for me.

If I let him in, I could be rejected.

If I let him in, he could reject my ideas, my dreams, my quirks, my beliefs, and my emotions. Once inside, he could reject the things I like to do, the love I have for my wife, the life I'm living, my tastes, my styles, and my favorite music and movies. Letting Andy in was going to put my life in front of him to see, taste, and smell and that was downright paralyzing. It was paralyzing to consider willingly putting my life in full view to be analyzed, examined, and dissected.

What will he think? What will he find? What about when I screw up? I'm sure I will. Over and over. And over. And over. And over, like a rock, rolling down the side of steep hill. You know, maybe somebody else should do this.

Maybe I ought to keep him on his side of the glass, while I stay on mine. I'll be the rare, endangered panda that he sees from a distance, but only a distance, because of course, I can't allow him to come in and disrupt my precious, natural habitat. *He can't be permitted to see what I do in my cave or what I'm like with the other pandas after zoo hours. That would screw everything up.*

He can be the zoo patron, prohibited from flash photography and getting too close.

Like a strobe light, the questions and the fears flashed in my mind, but the way I saw it I had no choice. Andy needed exactly what I needed from Chip all those years ago. So I welcomed him into my world beyond Texas barbeque.

I told him my story of growing up in the Christian shoebox, about why that was hard, about what I sensed God was doing in my life now, and why that was both pretty and challenging. I brought him into my home to spend time with Kristen and me, to see us kiss hello, laugh with each other and cry together, disagree, and to see me quote lines from *Anchorman* and then watch my wife roll her eyes.

Andy came out with my friends, to see our interactions, to see us encourage one another, act sarcastically with each other, and to see us obsess over fantasy football. In my work environment he saw me in moments of conflict, joy, and anger. He saw pictures of my family and when my mom flew in from Chicago, Andy was one of the first to meet her. What began as one lunch meeting slowly evolved into a fragrant relationship and through the subsequent months I watched something special happen.

Andy's heart began to soften.

Andy began to seek God for himself, to explore him, and as Andy drew closer and closer to God, he revealed himself more and more to Andy, and as he did Andy continued changing. He began to fall in love with Jesus, with the idea of giving his life away to others, and with grace. His belief that a relationship with Jesus is just that, and not just a convenient way for Christians to explain it, strengthened, and as it did, his skepticism towards God and his followers continued to fade. Soon he began volunteering in his church and investing his life into other people. After nearly a year, Andy was an intern, teaching within his community and leading teams of volunteers.

Today, God continues working something special through him, bringing change through him, and I couldn't be prouder to call Andy a great friend, a partner in ministry, and the most ardent lover of Jesus that I've ever seen. He believes and knows that God is everything that he hoped for, and more.

We still spend all sorts of time together and he often tells me that the greatest thing I offered him was simply an invitation into my life, to see it. Now if I could only get him to wear looser fitting jeans I'd be all set.

Death to Champions

Stripping Down to Real Living

I have an interesting relationship with sports. I really enjoy watching them, maybe a little too much, but it takes a specific set of circumstances for me to enjoy playing them. It makes sense though, I suppose. As a spectator, I can get mad when the athletes can't do things that, from my couch, seem so simple—things that, from my couch, I'm quite sure I could do just as well, if not better. As a spectator, I can pretend that I'm just as good as the athletes that I'm watching. As a participant, I'm reminded, very clearly, that in reality, I'm not. I'm reminded why they're playing, and I'm watching. One of my favorite sports to watch is college basketball.

One evening I was watching a particularly intense college basketball game, and as the seconds ticked away, players gasped for air, hunched forward on their sweaty knees, and guzzled cups of water. As it all unfolded, one of the announcers declared, "Champions never show weakness."

He didn't say, "Champions have no weakness." He said champions never *show* weakness.

So according to this announcer, champions feel the shooting pain of a sprained ankle rising through the back of their leg, just like everyone else, but unlike most, champions don't grimace. Champions get winded, just like everyone else, but they refuse to place their arms above their heads to draw air into their empty lungs like an ordinary person would. Champions feel the weight of pressure in the closing seconds, just like everyone else, but they hide that speck in their eye that tips everyone off. Champions have weakness, but they never show it, which makes champions masterful at hiding weakness and vulnerability.

After reflecting for a few moments, I realized something.

You know, if I use his philosophical insight as a lens through which to see my generation, then we're chock-full of champions. I'm a champion. So is he. And she is too. I guess most of us are.

I sing.

We are the new champions.

We are the new champions.

Me. And my friends.

Sure, we wave the banner of authenticity.

We prefer the wounded and rugged vigilante to the polished idol. We gravitate toward the dark heroism in the Christian Bale version of Batman over the Michael Keaton days, and we like the loose cannon 007 of Daniel Craig to the pristine, suave Bond of Pierce Brosnan. We say we want to be real and vulnerable, that we want to show who we really are, scars, weaknesses, and all. We claim we want to be genuine and we do, desperately, but that desire rarely seems to go beyond our faded jeans, singer-songwriter music, and taste in urban interior design.

Looking around, I see the weak pretending to be strong, the uncertain pretending to be confident, the lonely pretending to have friends, and the ignorant pretending to know the answer; I see smiles masking anger, laughter covering tears, and whispers burying screams. I hear things like, "Seriously, I'm fine" and "No, really. It's no big deal." So while we may want real, it seems that we are anything but real.

Toby the Champion

I sat on the cool stone steps, looking out over the lake. The water was dark and motionless, an aqua goddess lying perfectly still, not wanting to be disturbed. Toby—a good friend of two years—sat next to me.

Toby has a roller skating heart. He's the type of guy that will meet every person in the room before I've had the chance to complete a conversation with just one. He's funny and warm, jolly even, and that's not a term I use flippantly. While I love Toby, our friendship in those first two years had grown about an inch deep, and I think an inch might be generous.

We talked about music, debated the supremacy of Chicago-style pizza and Philly cheesesteaks, and laughed together, but if the conversation ever shifted to anything of a personal nature, Toby shut down. He wouldn't talk about his parents' divorce or about how his mom left him. He wouldn't talk about his struggles and sins, his fears, or his doubts. He wouldn't talk about hurts, deep hurts that left more scars on his heart than he could count. He wouldn't talk about or let anyone into any of it.

Conversations about any of those areas would reveal that he was less than perfect, that he had weakness, pain. They would reveal that Toby was still in process, and he didn't want that. He didn't want anyone to know what he was hiding, the secret wounds and uncertainties that hung over him every single day of his life. In fairness, few of us do because we know all too well that our world doesn't fancy the weak, the vulnerable, the ugly, and the broken.

We live in a world that embraces people who ride roller coasters and perform karaoke with no inhibitions, people who make bold, bright fashion statements and embark on entrepreneurial efforts. Our world French-kisses the strong and beautiful, the courageous and unafraid, the together and the self-assured, so we typically resist the moments, conversations, and experiences that may reveal us to be something else. And while this might not sound like too big of a deal, nothing could be further from the truth. While concealing weakness and vulnerability in the athletic arena makes sense and benefits both the competitor and the goal, living our lives with a champion's mentality, wearing a mask and costume as if we're attending the Capulet ball, only destroys us in the arena of life. To hide is to die. So without being real, without authenticity, there is no healing.

Healing comes through transparent, intimate relationships, both with God and others. It comes through sharing weakness, through confessing sin and laying all our cards on the table in accountability. It comes as we make ourselves vulnerable enough to receive support in the place we need it most. Authenticity is something we all need, but it's also something we can seldom create in someone else.

A great deal of what spawns authentic living are the things we don't have power over. They are the things that God, or life in general, sets in motion. I'm referring to conditions like "hitting bottom," breaking after years of bending, losing something, or losing someone. Usually, these things have nothing to do with us.

However, there is that rare role we can play in the lives of others, which leads me to my friend Isaac.

A Front Man, an Overeaters' Meeting, a Catalyst

Isaac is the front man of a '90s cover band.[1] They do everything from Boyz II Men, to Green Day, to Meat Loaf, to Hootie and the Blowfish. While they're on stage, he adopts an alter ego, another kind of persona that remains hidden the other six days of the week. He drapes himself in flannel, grabs the air with his hands, and kicks his ordinarily inflexible legs cheerleader high. It's a side project for him and he's great at it, but that's not why I mention him now.

I mention him because Isaac is one of my heroes and one of the most authentic people I know. He's the guy that *will* tell you in full detail how he is doing if you want to know. He doesn't pretend to know things, and his refusal to act okay when he isn't is like a cool rain in the middle of an Austin summer. Isaac walks the way not of a champion but of a loser.

Over one of our many lunches, I asked him how he was. Setting down his chilled Diet Dr Pepper, he said, "Josh, you know what I did yesterday?"

My eyebrows raised. I waited.

"I went to an Overeaters Anonymous meeting."

"What? Really?" It caught me off guard. "What was that like?"

"Well, to be honest, it was really awkward. I was the only guy there and the rest were forty-year-old soccer moms. I hated it, and when everyone took out their lunches, and I had to watch them eat, I hated it even more. But I needed to go. Josh . . . I'm depressed. And even though I know it's not going to help, I deal with it by eating. When I feel like crap, I don't feel like praying or reading my Bible, or talking about it. I feel like eating, so I eat."

At first I was kind of surprised, then a little uncomfortable, and then I sat in pure awe and admiration. Isaac is always honest about his wounds and warts. He doesn't hide the fact that he's broken. As I look at his life and the ways God uses him to bring change, his authenticity practically forces me to say, *Surely God is working through him, because there's no way someone that screwed up could do all that he does. And man, is he screwed up.*

He was and always is just Isaac, and I've seen how his way of stripped leading serves to promote real living in others.

People confess sin to Isaac. People weep with Isaac. When people hit bottom, they share it with Isaac. People stop hiding when they're around Isaac.

His authenticity gives others permission to be in process, to admit they need to grow. His authenticity allows others to say, "Yeah, me too," and that is one of the most powerful phrases in the English language. We say it when we realize we have company in our struggle and pain. His authenticity brings people out of the fake world, and if we are going to bring others out of the fake world, then maybe we have to live like Isaac. Maybe we have to be open about our sin, our struggles, and our pain with those around us. Maybe, in order to bring about authenticity in someone else, we have to be real.

That's hard for me. For a couple of different reasons.

First, it's hard because a lot of days, I want to be an icon. There is this part of me that wants to be admired and revered for how strong and holy I am, like I'm some sort of Christian celebrity. Because of that, I often don't live so that God will be honored and loved, but that I might be. Sometimes I actually catch myself roaming into a world of dreams, a world where I dream about others dreaming about me.

People hang posters of me on their walls and clamor for my approval and autograph. They brag if they see me around town. My picture is on lunchboxes and T-shirts. People talk about me. All of them. They know me. I am known. It's Friday night, and the world is watching Josh. There he is!!

Josh! Josh! Flashbulbs pepper the atmosphere. Snap! Snap! Snap! Screaming ensues. Maybe even some fainting. It's all-out hysteria! Pandemonium!

I'm on a higher plane. I am a plane. I'm flying. I'm an icon, living 30,000 feet above everyone else.

It's really hard for me to live and lead openly stripped and broken because I like that iconic idea a little too much, I think—usually too much to be anything less.

Second, it's hard because I feel like no one is expected to be a champion as much as a Christian is. Sometimes I feel as though I'm supposed to be a white knight, the flawless combination of Christopher Reeve's Superman and Oprah. Because I'm a Christian, I can't be feeble, vulnerable, in need of help, questioning or doubting God. Christians don't do that. And even if I am, I definitely can't bare it to others. There is just no room for that.

For so long, that's what I believed, and when I met Darren I found that he believed it too.

Enough Icons, Enough Superman

We crossed paths at a conference in New Mexico. He was kind of shy, and he wore a leather jacket. I don't know why I remember that about him. I guess I just don't see that many guys wearing leather jackets anymore. He wore one.

"Josh, what do you do when someone you are doing life with, or leading, walks away from you because of a mistake you made?"

Apparently, within the community he was leading, Darren had an ongoing relationship that had recently crumbled because of a mistake he made, leaving both him and the other individual wounded. This wasn't a case of marital infidelity, moral turpitude, or any other act that traditionally removes one from leadership, but it was, nevertheless, a mistake, and in response this individual chose to terminate the relationship.

Situations like Darren's are bound to happen if you live or lead long enough, but they still make me cringe. People can and will choose to walk away from relationships for all sorts of reasons, but knowing that doesn't take the sting out of it.

Wanting to give Darren some guidance, and knowing there wasn't much of a silver lining to offer, I posed this question: "I don't know, Darren. But, just out of curiosity, when is the last time you told this person about an area of weakness or sin in your life?"

After a pause, he said, "Never."

Never.

I rubbed my forehead, thumbing it hard, shifting and wrinkling my skin into ridges and aisles. At that moment, I probably looked more English bulldog than man. Then I looked at Darren and wondered if this individual walked away from Darren not because of his mistake but because he led him/her to expect perfection, because Darren wasn't willing to take him/her out of that champion's lifestyle and into real living. And beyond that I wondered how many Christians would issue the same response to that question as Darren. I still wonder that today and the answer, I'm afraid, is too many. And until we stop pursuing icon status and do away with the notion that Christians are supposed to be champions, we will all, Christians, my generation, and the world at large, continue the descent into the world of fake, because the only people that can serve as catalysts for others' authenticity are those like Isaac, who are willing to be authentic.

Living like Isaac is a constant wrestling match for me. I want to do it. I don't want to do it. I do it. I don't do it. It's scary and it's hard, but I can tell you that when I do, when I am willing to live and lead stripped, I experience and see the deep healing that happens. Both in me and in those around me.

The Death of Fakeness

My father passed away in June 2007 after a long battle with just about everything. Let me explain what I mean by that.

I don't remember a lot of the specific prognoses, detailed conversations with doctors, and medical jargon, but I remember how all of those moments, words, sicknesses, and procedures affected my life and family and stole so many of the things I enjoyed. I remember how they changed my relationship with my Dad.

Here's how I remember my Dad's medical history.

1940   Welcome to this world, James E. Riebock.

1950s James begins drinking.

1960s James continues drinking. And drinking.

1972   James E. Riebock has first heart attack. More drinking.

1979   I'm born. Congratulations, James!

1986   Dad throws the football with me often.

1987   Dad goes to AA and stops drinking.

1988   Dad still isn't drinking, but work has become his new beer. He does it all the time.

1989   Dad doesn't throw the football with me very much anymore.

1991   Dad is diagnosed with Parkinson's disease.

1992   Breathing is a struggle for Dad. Less throwing football.

1993   Dad is undiagnosed with Parkinson's disease. The doctor made a mistake the first time.

1994   Dad has second heart attack, no more throwing the football.

1994   Dad is going to die, so say what you need to say.

1994   Dad receives a heart transplant.

1996   Dad struggles going up the stairs, so if we're going to talk I have to go to his room.

2000   Dad has arthritis and walks with a cane.

2001   Dad begins falling down a lot.

2003   Dad is re-diagnosed with Parkinson's disease. This time he really has it.

2004   Dad has brain surgery and doesn't remember a lot of the things he used to.

2004   Dad is going to die, so say what you need to say.

2005   A shunt is placed in Dad's head.

2005   Dad is going to die, so say what you need to say.

2006   Dad can't walk anymore and only eats mashed-up food.

2006   Dad goes into the hospital and never comes home again.

As I said, he had a long battle with just about everything, and eventually, he just didn't want to fight anymore, so he checked himself into hospice. It was obvious his time to leave this world was near, but still, no one knew exactly when it would happen.

For days I sat perched in hospital chairs, consuming cups of stale coffee, yearning to see any sign of hope. Less coughing. Slightly pinker cheeks. A mildly increased appetite. A few times I'd swear I saw something positive, but remembering why I was there always yanked me back to reality and bankrupted any hope of his recovery. I was there to watch my dad die.

A week later, he did.

Right away, I missed his encouraging phone calls and hearing him say, "I'm proud of you," and his humor, though often predictable and borderline annoying, was suddenly something that I didn't know how I was going to live without. It's funny how all the things I so badly wanted to go away while he was alive were things I so badly wanted to have back now that he was gone. As you'd expect, losing my dad was hard and it was horrible, and it left me hurting, but I hid it well.

People would ask how I was doing, and my response always sounded strong and jammed with spiritual maturity. I would say something about only being concerned for my sisters, God having a plan, or how God was merciful in taking him. Those kinds of statements made me look really grounded and together—like a champion—and masked what was really going on in me.

I'm good at masks. I'm good at fake. I always have been.

Growing up in an alcoholic family, I learned how to fake it from the time I was a kid. I was taught how to smile through pain and act as if my family was as it should be.

What do you mean? My parents get along great! No, my dad's just tired right now. That's why he won't throw the football with me.

Everything's fine.

So projecting an image that I can handle anything, keep my head above water, and go with whatever comes, even when I can't, is a piece of cake. Too bad fakeness isn't a spiritual gift. If it were, I'd be in high demand.

Soon after Dad's passing, my sisters and I took Mom out for margaritas to celebrate Dad's life and also the new life that Mom now had ahead of her. In a way, Mom was given new life through Dad's death because she no longer had to care for him, which she had done for well over a decade. Her life was constant 911 calls, emergency rooms, stress, worry, medical bills, and trips to the pharmacy. His health was a burden not only for him but for her too, so when Dad died, that massive weight was lifted, and that was cause for all of us to celebrate and imagine what life was going to be like for her now.

We talked about her moving into a new house and decorating it just the way she wanted. We talked about her dreams of vacationing in South America and Europe. We even discussed her potentially dating again. This incredibly dynamic, flamboyant, and influential hippie theologian, my mom, was now going to live again. She would experience and shape the world in ways far beyond what her previous years had allowed. It was kind of poetic, really.

Ten weeks later, Mom died.

Liver transplants are supposed to be routine, they say, but this time it wasn't. While operating, the surgeons stumbled upon previously undetected terminal cancer that had spread throughout her entire body, and that was it. She died on the table. Weeks earlier she was healthy, or so it seemed, and then as a cloud of smoke disappears from a freshly used ashtray, she was gone.

Puff.

My family and I received the crushing news in a consultation room. My younger sister curled up on the chair next to me and cried softly. My older sister's loud sobs were interrupted by convulsions, which were interrupted when she collapsed to the floor, wailing uncontrollably. My wife hardly moved, except to put her hands over her face.

Me? I stood up and punched the wall as hard as I could. I showed my bones no mercy. Knuckles throbbing. Wrist aching. Taking a deep breath, I gently pressed my hands against the baby blue wallpaper, clenching my eyes closed, emotion bubbling to the surface. I was about to lose it, and I knew it, but I didn't want everyone to see me when I did, so I exited the consultation room and crossed the hallway, locking myself in the men's bathroom. The instant the deadbolt wedged into place, the tears flooded from my eyes. I sobbed. And I sobbed. And I sobbed, to the point where I grew nauseous, like I was going to vomit, homesick for the life I knew five minutes earlier. My knees grew weak, and I collapsed over the toilet, hugging the porcelain bowl, staring blankly into the water and dry heaving. Then I toppled backwards into the corner against the cold tile floor. I sobbed some more there.

Now propped against the wall and hysterical, I made a phone call to my friend, Andrew.

"Josh? Is that you?"

I didn't say anything. Just cried.

"Josh? What? What is it? What happened? What?"

"She died," I said, barely getting the words out between breaths.

"What?"

"SHE'S DEAD!" I yelled this time, sobbing some more.

"What?!"

"SHE'S DEAD!! MY MOM'S DEAD!!"

"What? Oh, my gosh!"

"I DON'T KNOW WHAT TO DO!! I CAN'T BELIEVE THIS! I just don't know what to do . . ."

"Oh, Josh. I'm so sorry. Oh, my gosh. OK, uh, I'm coming to the hospital. Oh, my gos—"

(Thump Thump Thump)

Someone began knocking at the bathroom door, so I hung up the phone. It was the hospital chaplain, asking if I was OK. I wasn't. That was the moment when I came undone, the moment when I unraveled, the moment when I completely fell apart, and on the floor of the Rush Hospital men's room, I directed all the anger, doubt, and pain of my scattered pieces squarely at God.

"F— YOU, GOD! F— YOU!! F—. . . How could you do this? How could you?! It wasn't enough to let my dad slip away? You had to take her too? Why? Why?! I'm so sick of you and your plans for my life! GET AWAY FROM ME!!"

I was so angry, all I felt was darkness, and God seemed far, far away. That didn't change in the coming days.

For weeks, I remained at a total loss for what to do, but being faithful to God wasn't high on my list. Actually, it wasn't really on my list at all. I guess I still knew he existed but in some ways that seemed trivial. What I wondered was if he cared.

Did God care that I was hurting?

I didn't know the answer to that question, or any of the other questions I had, but I knew the pain was real, and that it was unbearable, and that I couldn't hide it or pretend to be strong any longer. I was too broken to act as if I knew what was happening in my life and as if I believed that everything was going to be okay. I was wounded. I was vulnerable, and for the first time . . . it was obvious to everyone.

In a way, and against my will, the death of my parents initiated the death of my fakeness. Hiding my weak and vulnerable heart, living like a champion, became suddenly impossible and utterly pointless, and a funny thing happened when it all went down, when I finally let others into my pain. I experienced love from people around me like I never had before, and that love was nothing short of life-saving.

Ted flew to Chicago to be with me, and Pat paid for my ticket when I had to reschedule my flights. Ben, Chris, and Jamie sent some of the most touching emails I've ever read, and the phone became a channel of encouragement thanks to Mateen, John, and Doug. Martha, Kim, Rich, and a host of others delivered meals and toilet paper to my door. Andrew drove to Ohio to pick up my grandmother so she could attend the funeral of her only daughter, which Chuck paid for. Ken, Margaret, Kori, and Matt cleaned my parents' house, and Kristen, Corbett, and Quinn listened as I expressed my anger, overwhelming grief, and confusion.

God used the love of so many to bring healing to my fractured heart, in ways both simple and complex. That love allowed me to get out of bed, to smile again, to feel cool breezes across my face, and to enjoy my wife's soft kisses again, but it also allowed me to love again, to move forward, and even to seek God again. And when I did, I experienced him like I never had before.

As I tiptoed back, God was somehow closer than ever, and the only rationale I can point to for it is that I finally engaged him with an uncensored honesty, and that's something I had never done. Prior to that time in my life, I thought God's greatest concern was what I come to him with, but what I found is that God's greatest concern is simply who I come to. He simply wants me to come to him. So I did. I came to God not as I "should" but as I was—not treating certain topics and emotions as off-limits, not pretending to be strong and composed and full of faith, but genuinely pissed off, confused, hurt, and overwhelmed with doubt, and I've come to believe that's what God really longs for.

He doesn't want the champion version of me. He wants the loser me. The authentic me. The unraveled, bathroom-floor version of me. He wants the real me. And he wants the real you.

He's not interested in our disguises, and it's when we approach God in honest weakness rather than fake strength that we experience him and his healing touch most powerfully. I certainly found this to be true, and in the coming months, God slowly restored me, tenderly whispering his honest promises of love and mercy, and inviting me to come to him with all of my true feelings and doubts, rather than leaving them at the door.

But in the midst of it all, I wasn't the only one God restored.

With Isaac's encouragement, I began sharing my story with others, complete with the confusion, grief, and what I now refer to as the "F.U. Moment." I spoke candidly about my anger toward God and areas of sin in my own life. My tireless reluctance to live authentically was greatly weakened, and the more I offered the real me and clung to a real God, the more others were able to take hold of him too, and as they did, I saw God bring change.

As I shared my brokenness, others responded by opening their doubt, hurt, and struggles to God and others, and as they did, God did his restoration thing. Bloody wounds, caused by children lost to diseases and failing battles with addiction, were expressed freely and honestly. Buried sin came to light for the first time, and I don't know how many times the phrases, "I've never talked about this before," or "Yeah, me too," were echoed.

It was absolutely beautiful, in a painful sort of way.

As I walked vulnerably, God took people by the hand and led them a few more paces out of the champion's world. One of those people was Toby.

That night, looking over the slumbering lake, I shared with him how hard it was for me to wade through pain over losing my parents. I cried, hard, the kind of crying where your body shakes and hurts afterwards. I shared my doubts about God, the difficult and seemingly answerless questions I was asking, and as I did, God broke through to Toby's heart.

"Josh, I don't understand."

He spoke quietly.

"What? What don't you understand?"

"Any of it. I don't get it."

"But which part?"

"I JUST DON'T UNDERSTAND, OKAY!!!"

"What, Toby?"

"I just don't understand how you can still want God in your life with all that's happened. Josh, he took your parents from you!! He took them!"

I didn't have a great theological response to offer him. All I had was honesty.

"I don't know, Toby. Actually, a lot of times I'm not really sure that I do trust him anymore. But I guess, when it really comes down to it . . . I don't think God did this to my family. I guess I think that this just happened, and I'm just trying to believe that he wants to love me now more than ever. And somehow, I think he does."

With that, the champion in Toby shrieked a dying cry, and Toby said, "Josh, I just don't think I can trust God."

Just so you know, those aren't bad words. Those are beautiful words. Powerful words. Honest words. Those are healing words.

From there Toby and I talked at length about his struggles to trust God and people, the deep and raw hurt he still felt from his parents' divorce, and at the end of our time, Toby asked me to pray for him, for his struggle to trust God and his pain, and I did. Then Toby prayed. Like the psalmist, he cried out to God for help, dumping on him his doubts and anger, and then he cried out to God on my behalf too—for my pain, my doubts, and my healing.

That night God brought Toby a little farther down that path of restoration, one that he is still walking today. Authenticity continues to grow in his spirit, and his healing continues. He, like so many others, not only needed to take that path, but he wanted to take that path. He just needed someone or something to take him there, and as it turned out, my greatest pain, my greatest weakness, was that thing. And the same may be true for you. Your greatest hurt, greatest failure, and greatest shortcoming may be what someone needs to come out of the champion's world and into the healing world of real living.

The only question is, are you willing to give it to them?

As a generation, we don't need more champions in our lives. We have plenty of those. The world has plenty of those. We need more people like Isaac, stripped people who are willing to lead others out of the world of fake. We want to be real. We want to strip off the coats of paint, and when someone is willing to take us there, we will follow and respond with screams of joy as we do.

25,000 Screams of Hope

Kristen and I went to a U2 concert in Milwaukee. It was raining hard outside—racehorse-sized drops utterly determined to flood. I only remember because we got soaked going into the stadium, so the entire show we were shivering, but it was incredible nonetheless.

Bono, The Edge, Larry, and Adam played most of the songs that I wanted to hear, including one that I didn't think they would play, "Who's Gonna Ride Your Wild Horses." From the album *Achtung Baby*, it was, for me, the most memorable song of the night for multiple reasons.

For one, Bono and The Edge played it by themselves. Sauntering, as giants, out to the front of the stage with only an acoustic guitar accompanying them, they began, and it was instantly and utterly mesmerizing, drawing the entire stadium into its melodic symphony.

But it's what transpired next that made the song eternally memorable.

With The Edge strumming and the stadium spinning in a hushed buzz, Bono began singing, shaking the arena with his street gospel voice. It was awesome. There was only one problem. He began singing at the wrong time.

As he swallowed the words, a look of confusion swelled across Bono's face. He glanced over to The Edge, who laughed and slowly shook his head.

"I'm sorry," said Bono in his sharp Irish accent, "I just messed up. We haven't done this one in a long time."

It was so honest. So real. He could have pretended he knew what he was doing or acted as though it was a rehearsed scene, but he didn't. Both he and The Edge chose to be losers rather than champions, and the instant his words hit the air, 25,000 people started screaming and cheering, louder than any other moment in the concert. And I don't think it was a malicious mob glorying in the blunder of the biggest rock band on the planet.

I like to think it was 25,000 prisoners releasing cheers of hope—hope that through the realness of someone else, they too might be set free to be real; hope that through the stripped life before them, they would no longer have to live like champions.

True Tales of a Lonely, Lonely People

And Why Family-Style Love May Be the Only Hope

The Tale of the Weeping Reaper and How He's Much Like Me

"Can I talk to you outside?" he asked in a rough and steely voice, triggering my immediate discomfort.

After I spoke at a church, the grim reaper approached me. He was a strange figure, much bigger than me, and very tall, with broad shoulders. He was draped in all black clothing and trailed by a death-stained mist. The part you might not expect is that the grim reaper had a very human name. His name was Jeremy.

"Sure, of course."

I reluctantly agreed to his request, and we stepped out into the dim parking lot, where he took from his pants a sickle-like heavy metallic lighter. Snapping it open, he calmly lit up a cigarette. As the first puffs of smoke hit the thick, humid air, he began to share.

"Josh, I found out today my girlfriend is pregnant."

His statement was stale, void of emotion, which I found curious even for someone like the reaper. Looking off behind me, he exhaled charcoal-colored smoke and continued, "But that's not what I want to talk to you about."

I stood there. And said nothing.

Jeremy inhaled and after a brief pause said, "I'm really caught up in drugs right now. I don't sell them, but I use them."

Again, stale, with no emotion. He blew the next round of smoke from his nostrils.

"But that's not what I want to talk to you about either."

What's next? I thought.

Maybe he shot JFK? That could be it. No it couldn't, not really. I know, maybe we're brothers separated at birth, like something out of a soap opera. Now that I look closer, we do have a similar nose. Kind of large. Very defined.

That's a dead giveaway.

But nothing could have prepared me for what was next.

"Josh. The first time I killed someone, I was fourteen years old."

At first, I wasn't sure if I believed him or not. Maybe I just didn't want to believe him because, if I did, that meant I had to do something, and I had no idea what to do and certainly no clue what to say.

No way. There's no way. What do I say to a murderer? To a cold-blooded killer? That's what he is! Cold as ice. Wait a minute, what is a cold-blooded killer going to say to me? Even worse, what is he going to do to me?

In that moment, shadows felt bigger, so big that I swear I could hear them breathing. Anxiety began to creep over me, and then Jeremy said, "I just feel so dead inside."

It was the first thing out of his mouth with the slightest hint of feeling, the first sign of any life. Jeremy threw down his flame-capped cigarette, and as he jammed his hands deeply into his pockets, his eyes became glassy, and he started to cry. My heart broke.

Jeremy wasn't a cold-blooded killer to me anymore, like he had been only moments earlier. He wasn't the grim reaper.

He was a wounded man, a hurting and vulnerable man, a man clinging to the thinnest thread of hope that someone, even someone that he had just met, would be willing to come into his messy life, to enter into his lonely and painful everyday existence, and not leave him to find his own way out of the darkness.

Standing there, I suddenly felt something that I wasn't expecting to feel with Jeremy. Commonality. In that moment, I felt like Jeremy and I had a lot in common. His life was a mess, there's no question about that, but so was mine. It was a different kind of mess, but no less of one. Messiness is one of those common threads that we all share. It's part of what it means to be human, and it always will be a part of it. To be human is to have sin, pain, and brokenness, so Jeremy and I had a lot in common. But there was a major difference between us.

I wasn't alone in my mess, but Jeremy was alone in his. While I had people who were willing to walk with me through the messiness, Jeremy didn't.

He was completely alone, plagued by seclusion. He was abandoned and forgotten. He lived in a heartbreaking world of everyday solitary confinement; a world of God-awful desperate isolation; a world where everyone was around him, but no one was there for him; a world where no one firmly took his hand and walked alongside him. He was an unworn prom dress, an abandoned gas station on a highly trafficked road, a lone peak, an unopened literary masterpiece, and a real-life, modern-day Eleanor Rigby.

All he wanted was to be accompanied in his mess, to be meaningful to someone else—so meaningful that they couldn't bear to leave him alone. And in that moment, I wanted so badly to be that someone for him. I wanted so badly to get messy with him, but every fiber of my selfish being fought against doing it and threatened to push me into the normal, ugly list of things I typically do.

Josh's list of selfish things to do
when a lonely person really needs love:

1. Come up with a convenient excuse why I can't be there for him
2. Ignore the person because her life is too messed up, or she's too different from me
3. Be nice to him, giving what I want to give, but never giving what he needs
4. Nod my head and say, "Man, that's tough," but avoid anything that will cost me emotionally, mentally, physically, or financially
5. Invite her to church, and pass her off to someone else ASAP
6. Tell him I'll pray for him, and maybe I will, but chances are I won't
7. Get really caught up in work and other things that I consider more important than a person who is so desperately lonely, the only friend they have is their imagination
8. Withhold any sacrificial act, anything that will be hard for me, and be sure to do only what will keep my life clean and easy
9. Stay involved in enough of my stuff that I never get involved in their stuff

Typically, my selfishness pushes me to love the people around me (Kristen, my sisters, my friends, acquaintances, random people in my building, waitresses, pretty much everyone) so poorly and so dimly, and sometimes to not love at all. It pushes me to make myself my primary concern, and as I let it push me around, others are left hurting, left to navigate their own pain, confusion, and sin alone. So as the tears fell down Jeremy's face, my selfishness, like always, pushed and pushed and pushed against me, but this time, for some reason, I pushed back.

I don't know what made this time so different. I suppose it's because this time I wasn't so blind, because this time I saw so much of myself in the other person, because I saw so much of myself in Jeremy, because I knew that the person throwing down that warm cigarette, bursting into tears, and hoping that someone would love enough to get messy, could easily be me tomorrow.

So I pushed back and did the only thing that felt remotely natural. I leaned in and I held him. I held Jeremy. And sitting on the curb with my arm around him, through the sobs, the snot, and the garglings, Jeremy rehashed for me his gang involvement and his all-important role of eliminating problem people.

Through the years, he had taken multiple lives, and in the process, his heart became numb, void of any sensitivity or feeling. That's why the news of his girlfriend's pregnancy could be taken without the slightest hiccup and why revealing that he had a drug problem was as routine as changing the radio station. His heart was in so much pain it didn't even feel any more.

Long into the night, Jeremy talked about the hurt, the mistakes, the regret, and worst of all, having to bear all of it alone.

I don't really remember how long we sat there, but I know that it was a long time. By the time we had prayed together, stood, and hugged, the night had grown much cooler and the parking lot was empty. Every car and every person were gone, but Jeremy's mess wasn't. It still remained. I didn't take it away or clean it up, but beginning that humid night it was no longer just his mess.

It was mine too.

A Tale of Two "Strangers," and How I Came to Believe That Their Story Is Essential to Our Healing

I was first introduced to the story of the Good Samaritan in Sunday school.

My teacher (one of the dads from the church, who, for some reason, always wore a brown suede jacket) liked to talk about it. Sometimes it felt like we talked about it every week and each time we did, at the conclusion of the story, he tried to motivate me to be nice to people, kind of like a holy Boy Scout. He wanted me to give homeless people a dollar, help little old ladies across the street, give my friends some of my Skittles, or things along those lines; and to a degree, that always made sense to me.

I believed that Jesus wanted me to do those things, to be nice, kind, and charitable, to give people some of my Skittles, but as I got older the story began to strike me as a little . . . stale—as kind of weak. I just didn't understand why Jesus needed to tell everyone to be nice to each other, when it seemed like such common sense. The story just didn't add up, that is, until I really looked at it for myself.

Around my early twenties, I think, I began to realize that there was much more depth to this story than I thought. I began to see that it was about much more than what my friend's dad in the brown suede jacket said. I began to see it as a very big and profound story—a very challenging, radical, and passionate story—with a very profound and radical God behind it.

Let me tell you the way I've come to see this story.

A Samaritan is traveling along the side of a cliff, on a rocky road. He's on his way to meet some friends that he's not seen in years. He's excited to laugh with them, tell stories, and point out how much each of them has aged since they last saw each other. He's riding his donkey.

He loves that donkey—not at all flashy or frilly, always reliable, and surprisingly comfortable for a stable animal. They have a special human-to-beast relationship.

"Aghh . . ."

Rounding the corner, with a smile on his face, the Samaritan hears a faint noise. Thinking very little of it, that it's only the sound of the wind through the bushes, he continues riding.

"Is—is someone there?"

That's not the sound of the wind and the Samaritan knows it. That's the sound of a person, a person who needs help.

"Whoa, boy," the Samaritan says to his donkey. "Whoa."

Propping himself up and looking over the front of his donkey's mane and head, he sees someone lying on the side of the road. The man is beaten badly. The Samaritan can hardly believe that he's alive, or that he will be much longer. His face looks like ground-up animal flesh, bloody and mangled, and his tunic is torn and dark crimson red. There's so much blood, it's difficult to tell which part of the body is which.

For a moment, the Samaritan pauses and thinks about his friends. He thinks about how much he wants to see them, to be with them. He thinks about how he wants to relax with them and eat with them. But his pause lasts only a moment. He knows they can wait. He knows they have to wait.

Leaping from his donkey, he runs to the beaten person, carrying with him a small bag.

"Yeah. Yeah. Someone's here. I'm here," he says.

81

"Pl-please. Help m-me. Don't leave me. Please, don't leave me here all alone."

The Samaritan kneels next to the bloody stranger.

"I won't. I'm gonna help you."

He takes from his bag a tiny, dusty vial. Removing the cork and taking the traveler's head in his right hand, he begins pouring oil and wine onto his wounds, gently wiping away the blood. He was saving these precious liquids for a special occasion, but what could be more special than a chance to save the life of another? Nothing.

As he continues to gently wipe the man's body with his bare hands, blood gives way to the color of flesh. He then bandages his wounds. The Samaritan knows that what he has done is good and true, but he also knows that it's not enough, so without hesitation, he slides his arms under the stranger's body, scraping them on the rocks. He braces himself and then lifts the stranger into his chest. The remaining blood smears across his cheek, down his arms, and across his tunic.

He's now covered in the blood of the stranger, covered in his pain, covered in his mud, covered in his mess.

With trembling steps, the Samaritan walks to his donkey. He gives his beast friend a look that says, "We have to do this for him. He needs us," and gently rests the stranger upon the gray animal. Climbing onto the donkey, the Samaritan slides the stranger onto his lap, as if holding a child, and begins to ride. As he does, he whispers, "It's gonna be okay. You're gonna make it. I'm right here. You're not alone anymore."

In the opposite direction of where his friends wait, he rides, holding the stranger on his lap. Every few miles, he stops to give him water, but also to ease the pain in his own back and neck. He's been carrying the stranger for miles, and it's taking its toll. Finally, after an exhausting ride, he arrives at an inn. It's not the cheapest inn he could find, but he's not looking for the cheapest. He's looking for a place that can provide what this stranger needs, and that's expensive. That will cost him.

He was saving this money to fix his roof. It leaks at night, making his bedroom cool and drafty, but this is more important. This stranger is more important. So he pays the innkeeper, and after carrying the stranger up the stairs, lays him down in the soft bed.

It's late now.

The sun is down and the Samaritan is tired. He's worn out, emotionally, physically, and financially, but he doesn't sleep. He sits at the foot of the bed where the beaten man lies and periodically checks on him, brings him water, and says, "You're not alone. I'm right here with you."

As the sun rises the next morning, the stranger sleeps, but the Samaritan doesn't. He's been awake all night, and now he has to go and let his friends know that he's okay. They'll be worried.

So he hands the innkeeper money, the very last of what he has, and tells him, "Look, I need you to take care of him for me. Don't leave his side. I've got to take care of a few things, but I'm coming back as soon as I get the chance. If he wakes up, please tell him I'll be back. Can you do that for me?"

"Okay, I will," says the innkeeper, as the Samaritan walks out the door. "But, wait a minute!"

The Samaritan stops and turns, looking into the face of the curious innkeeper.

"Why are you doing this? You don't even know this guy. You don't know anything about him. He's a total stranger."

"No," the Samaritan says, "he's not. He's much more than that."

To me, that's the story of the Good Samaritan now.

It's no longer that small story that I learned as a kid. It's not a story about being nice or Secret Santas. It's not just a story about a guy who, out of naive kindness, helped someone. It's so much more than that.

It's the story of an individual who treats a stranger as something more. It's the story of an individual who sees and treats a lonely, messy person like he's a member of his own family. It's the story of a person who is willing to do whatever it takes for the sake of another. It's the story of a different love, of a bigger love, of a brighter love. It's the story of Christ's love, true love, and there's nothing stale or weak about it.

This story speaks to a longing deep within my heart.

I want what this story talks about, because in many ways, I'm just as beaten, messy, and alone as that wounded traveler. So I don't want another person who will just be nice to me, another person that will know my phone number, another person that will be there for me every now and again, or another person that will love me in small, painless, low-cost ways.

No, I want a big love, a love that tells me I'm "more than that" to someone. I want to be loved like family. I want to know that I won't be left alone in my mess, that I have a place to belong, and that when I hurt, someone will be there to hurt with me. I want to know that someone will give to me without asking for anything in return, that someone will tell me what I need to hear even when it'll hurt, and that I won't just have people around me, but that I'll have people who are there for me.

I want that. I need that.

At the end of the day, I think, as a generation, we all do.

Maybe that's why Jesus tells us to go and do likewise.

The Tale of the New Roommate

On a winter evening, when the ground wasn't as soft and the air had grown a tad biting, Blake came over for dinner.

Kristen and I met her years earlier at a church, where she was leading worship. We liked her immediately and became friends, friends that spoke often, but when she moved away for college, we heard from her less and less. We called her, emailed her, and text messaged her, but rarely heard anything back. She became something of a phantom to us. It wasn't because Blake suddenly disliked us, but because she had fallen on hard times, and into hard things.

Early on in her college experience, drugs became a part of her life, and soon after, while at a party, she was raped. She didn't know who it was, or why he had picked her, but for some reason, he did. Through the rape, she became pregnant and shortly after, she had the baby aborted. After that, her life spiraled totally out of control.

Drugs became a bigger and bigger part of it, as did casual sex. She turned her anger and pain at God, pushing him away and toying with spirit channeling. She stopped nearly all communication with anyone that cared about her, and continued to surround herself with people that didn't, people that only wanted her for their purposes, people that surrounded her but weren't really there. So when she arrived in her fifth year of college, her life was a complete mess, and she was all alone in it. But that winter day, I received a very pleasant surprise, a text message from Blake.

Wat u guys doin 4 dinner?

[Translation: What are you guys doing for dinner?]

Hopflly eating w u. Com ovr!

[Translation: Hopefully eating with you. Come over!]

☺

[Translation: Okay! What time should I come over? I can't wait to see you guys! And thank you!]

A few hours later, Blake walked through the door. We sat down together for Chinese take-out and got each other up to speed on what had been happening in our lives. Then, I got to be a part of a conversation that I'll remember forever.

"So, Blake, really, how are you? I mean, I can't imagine going through all that you've been through, both the stuff that happened to you and the stuff that you had some control over. So how are you?" Kristen asked.

"Yeah, not so good . . . I want to get out of this life I'm in so bad, but I just don't know how to start. I don't know what to do. I mean, I'm at the bottom, and I just don't know how to get out."

"Blake, I know it might feel like the bottom, but did you ever think that maybe it isn't?" I asked. "To me, that's the scariest part about all of this—maybe it can get worse."

Blake didn't say anything, and I continued.

"The truth is, if you aren't willing to make some real changes, it probably will get worse, and then you will hit the bottom . . . and I'm afraid of what that might be."

She looked down at the table.

"Maybe you're right"—her voice was somber—"but I just feel like there's no way out of this. I'm trying to get out of all the drug stuff, I just want to graduate, I know I need people that love me and I know I need God in my life again, but I'm living with a guy that sells LSD and smokes weed all day. I've got no one, it's like I'm stuck . . ."

"Blake," Kristen said, looking over at me. "This is probably one of the times where I should talk to my husband before I say something, but I'm going to say it anyway. You need to move in with us. And I want you to move in with us. We can't fix everything, and we definitely don't have a lot of space. But we want to be there for you in any way we can be."

It was one of those moments that so indelibly reminded me of why when I began dating Kristen, I couldn't stand to let her go. We only dated for six weeks before I told her that I loved her. Some people might call this premature, but those people don't know what had happened in my heart. I loved her, and I knew it, so I told her. Her response was one of complete honesty. She simply said, "I know." A few weeks later, she reciprocated the words back to me, and after six months, we were engaged. From the beginning of our relationship, she showed me what love looks like, and that's only continued through the course of our marriage.[1] I was drawn to the way she loved so many people then, and I'm drawn to her loving way of life now. To me, the way she lives is not only how Christ lived, but also why Christ lived.

He came to be Emmanuel, God with us. God involved. God in the mess. He lived to enter our lives and get our mess on him, and he did. The cross is, of course, a vividly violent picture of this. On the cross, along with his own pain, Christ took and felt ours. He felt the shame and guilt of our sin. He put our mess on him, he got messy, and though we weren't created to clean up anyone's mess, we are created to reflect Christ by entering the lives of others and getting messy. That's exactly what Kristen does, and in that moment, it's exactly what she did. She decided that we were going to step into Blake's life and get messy.

"Wow. I don't know," Blake said. She looked even more stunned than I was. "Josh, are you okay with that?"

"Yeah, I am. I don't know how it'll all work, but of course I am. We love you and we want you here," I said.

Blake's eyes brightened.

"Oh my God, you guys. Okay. I will . . . I'm so excited right now."

The next morning, we picked up Blake's things and moved her into our 900-square-foot, one-bedroom, one-bathroom condo, and for the next four weeks, she lived with us, and I got to see, through Kristen, a clearer and clearer picture of what love really looks like.

Sure, Kristen and Blake did the normal things that people who live together do, things like watching movies, walking the dog, eating, meeting other friends, and talking of relationships, God, hurt, church, and worst dates ever. But there was more to it than that.

Kristen did Blake's hair and let Blake do hers. Kristen gave Blake rides to and from places she needed to be and let Blake borrow her clothes. Kristen held Blake as she wept about her past decisions, her pain, the rape that happened through no fault of her own, and the fact that no one really knew her. And sometimes, Kristen wept with her. Every night as Kristen came to bed, she stood in the doorway and told Blake, "We're so glad that you're here."

One night, at around 12:15 a.m., Blake and I were watching a movie. I was tired and beginning to fade, when the front door burst open. Kristen walked in with another girlfriend, carrying a birthday cake with twenty-three candles, lit and burning. It was Blake's birthday. Kristen remembered and made sure to celebrate it.

Over and over, I saw through Kristen what messy family love looks like, and I got to see how God uses it to change lives. Following the end of Blake's time living with us, she sent Kristen and me a letter, thanking us and expressing her love for each of us. Here's a portion of it.

Kristen, what can I say? What can I say to one of the people that literally saved my life? I know that sometimes people say that to sound extreme, but it really isn't. These past couple of weeks have been the happiest and hardest of my life. Recently, all I have known are people who think the worst of me, people who would rather leave me than take me, but you opened your arms and took me in. You didn't "witness" to me or shove Christ down my throat. You didn't treat me as an object, but like a member of your own family. You showed me a love from a God that I now know I can't live without, and life isn't over for me. Thank you so much for loving me when no one else would. You've changed my life.

As of today, Blake is drug free, talking to God again, reading a Bible again, believing in herself again, believing in love again, and finding healing.

She's no longer alone.

The Tale of the Dead Serious Reminder

NOTHING CAN REPLACE LOVE
  NOTHING WAS MEANT TO REPLACE LOVE
NOTHING CAN REPLACE LOVE
  NOTHING WAS MEANT TO REPLACE LOVE
NOTHING CAN REPLACE LOVE
  NOTHING WAS MEANT TO REPLACE LOVE
NOTHING CAN REPLACE LOVE
  NOTHING WAS MEANT TO REPLACE LOVE

Like Jeremy, the beaten traveler, Blake, Eleanor Rigby, and even sometimes me, my generation is gruesomely lonely, but in response, we don't need another handout, another kind gesture, or a better Bible study. We don't need more people that will merely know our name and address or care for us sporadically and at arm's length.

We need big, reimagined, Jesus kind of love, and people willing to sacrifice themselves in order to live it with us. We need people who will love us enough to get messy.

So be deeply involved. Be covered in someone's tears. Be the person who gets the call at midnight. Be the person who hears the gory details when someone's marriage or career falls apart. Be the person who tells someone the hard stuff that they need to hear but no one wants to say. Be the person who repeatedly gets someone else's mud and blood all over you. Be the person who goes home a little uncomfortable at night, not because of your behavior and thoughts, but because you've been near enough to someone else's.

Be a family member to the lonely, messy people of this world, and to my generation.

The Graceless Stampede

And Living alongside Those Who Have Been Trampled

Shortly after Kristen and I moved to Austin, Tyson and Anna moved into the apartment below us. They, like us, had recently married and migrated south in search of warmer weather; while we left Chicago, they left big-city New York. Anna was a glamorous, Hollywood kind of gorgeous, witty, and had a great sense for fashion. Tyson was a big-time corporate manager for Home Depot. He's the savvy and charismatic type, really smart with a little bit of a young George Clooney look. He loved talking sports and relaxing by the pool. That's all the two of us needed to begin a friendship.

One particular evening, with Anna out of town, the three of us went out to a swanky Austin seafood restaurant for dinner. It was one of those places where the waiters and waitresses drape a white napkin over their stiffly postured arm and address everyone, even if it's little kids, as "Sir" or "Ma'am." Following discussions about the most effective strategies to quit smoking and why the New York Mets ownership is incompetent, Tyson began to ask questions about my beliefs—specifically, about my beliefs in God.

"Josh, what's your take on God? I mean, what do you think he's really like?"

"Well, I don't know, it depends on what you mean. I believe in God, if that's what you mean. And I believe that he's . . . misunderstood a lot of the time."

"What do you mean?" Tyson asked.

"Well, I think God is much more loving and personal than we often think. I don't believe that God is so far that I can't touch him."

"Hm." Tyson nodded and set his glass down. "I believe some of that too. By any chance, are you Christian?"

"Well, depending upon how you define that, yeah, I—" I said, before Tyson interjected.

"You know what I hate about Christians?"

Maybe I'm a masochist or a glutton for punishment, but for some reason, I love it when people jumpstart sentences that way. At least it's honest, and most of the time I agree with the words that follow.

"They are so damn judgmental."

He stated it firmly, with an apologetic twinge, and while I was saddened to hear him say it, I wasn't at all surprised. That accusation is thrown in the direction of Christianity all too often, and yet I think our immediate response is often to raise our arms and refute it, as if it's a thing of the past . . .

The year is 1879 and Rutherford B. Hayes is President of the United States. The entire southwest territory is a wild place, overrun with outlaws, vagabonds, whores, and thieves. But one town remains free of scum.

Welcome to Gaveltown
Population: 6999
"The most moral of people
and staunchest enforcers of it"

Scum steer clear of Gaveltown. None are daring enough to even set foot in the hotel for an evening of rest or the general store for a box of fresh cigars. They'd rather face a Federal Marshall and his smoking pistols than the weapons of this town: words, glances, and opinions. Here, folks fight with them, and there's nothing deadlier in the entire southwest. Here, scum don't stand a chance.

Here in Gaveltown, they let scum know just exactly what they are, and what they always will be.

If only Gaveltown were a place of the past, this world would be so different. But it's not. Gaveltown is close. It's now. It's much of the world, and the Christianity, in which we live.

So please, let me save you what could be time and energy spent doing something more productive and assure you— Tyson's ghastly statement is largely and sadly true, especially in our eyes, the eyes of my generation. To us, harsh judgment is as constant within Christianity as Norm Peterson in the bar on *Cheers*.[1] As I leaned forward in my chair, Tyson shared with me the story (there's always a story) behind his firm perception.

Not Just Another Pesky Gnat

Years earlier, his brother-in-law, a pastor, began heaping judgment upon him and Anna for sleeping together before they were married and for not adhering to the ways of Jesus. He made definitively negative statements about Tyson's character and told him multiple times, straight up, "Tyson, you're going to hell!"

Hearing Tyson share, in detail, the severity of the comments only crystallized how harsh it really was.

I don't need, nor would it be beneficial, to go into all the specifics about what transpired between him and his brother-in-law, but take a wild guess. What do you think an evangelical pastor might say to the guy who is sleeping with his younger sister? It was nasty, and it hurt Tyson a great deal.

Judgment hurts because it isn't just a pesky gnat with an inconvenient sting. Judgment is a stampede that mercilessly tramples already broken souls, leaving victims crushed under massive weights of guilt, fear, and rejection while thundering the message, "YOU AREN'T ACCEPTED HERE! YOUR SIN IS TOO MUCH TO OVERCOME!" This kind of judgment is deadly, and many of us have been on the receiving end of it.

Matt is a southerner from Atlanta, Georgia, so he has one of those really cool accents that everyone else wishes they had, that I wish I had. The only people with a cooler accent than a Georgian accent are from Boston, Australia, Scotland, Italy, and some parts of England.

So Matt has that going for him.

We met in college as next-door neighbors and it took all of five minutes to discover that he was a connoisseur of college weekend culture. Translation: he was big into the party scene. And I mean big. Picture an athletic version of John Belushi from *Animal House*. At the party, he wasn't the shirtless guy doing the keg stand and persuading all others to partake in the ancient ritual of the beer bong; he was the guy standing on the roof donning nothing but a Confederate flag as a cape while doing both of those things.

So on most weekends, and even some weeknights, while I wrapped up marathon video game sessions (Nerd Alert) in the wee hours of the morning, Matt was just returning from a raucous party or strip club, where he may or may not have gotten into a fist fight.

One night in particular, while Matt and I lived together as roommates, he stumbled through the front door of our cramped, boy-dirty dorm room, drunk and crying. The tears were not prompted by anything of the tragic variety, he just happened to get really emotional when enough alcohol to kill an elephant streamed through his veins. Awakened by Matt's gentle sobs and the intermittent sound of his vomiting both on the floor and on himself, I helped him undress—first his dressy button-down shirt, followed by his fancy leather shoes and crisp country club pants. For the next few hours, I emptied the wastebasket each time it filled with whatever food Matt had eaten earlier that day, and I simply sat with him. All night, we sat on the couch, and throughout the entire ordeal, he reiterated over and over how much he loved me, and assured me that I was the only person that cared about him.

I've been told that people are at their most honest when they are drunk, and though at the time it was kind of funny bumping into Matt's emotional and mushy side, looking back, it doesn't seem funny because he probably meant every word of it. I think those words were born out of a place a little closer to Matt's heart than I realized. I think Matt really believed that I was the only person who cared about him. The community around him certainly wasn't a haven of support and care.

His struggles were reason enough for most to dissociate from him or reject him outright. Sometimes, during conversations on stained dorm couches, my college mates would mention Matt's name, often spewing poison and carrying on with all sorts of rumors and allegations against him.

"I just can't see why anyone would hang around him. Do you?"

"He's just dirty."

"He's the kind of guy that would rape a girl. I know he would."

"I'll bet he has some kids he doesn't know about. But what's the difference? He wouldn't take care of them anyway!"

"It's simple. He's a bad guy."

"What makes him most pathetic is that he's fine with his drinking problem. I'll bet he likes being an alcoholic."

"He doesn't care about anyone but himself, and he never will."

If you listened long enough, you had a hard time distinguishing where the boogeyman ended and where Matt began, and while he had his struggles and problems, he was anything but a monster. Walking with God wasn't a way of life for him, but he never claimed it was, and unlike many Christians I knew, I found Matt to be acutely self-aware and genuine about his own shortcomings and brokenness. He was, just like you and me, in need of repair and seeking acceptance. Actually, he still is.

About a year ago, after not seeing each other since college, I saw Matt again. We had dinner together, and it was great to catch up, reminisce about the old days, and hear that cool Georgian accent. He sells air conditioners, and he likes it, on most days. He lives on the east coast now and is still a bit of a college party guy. We talked for a long time, and as we did, it became clear that Matt still drags shame, guilt, and fear everywhere he goes.

"So, you still into Jesus?"

"Yeah, I am," I said, nodding my head. "What about you? You interested in any of that right now, Matt?"

"Nah, man. I haven't really had much to do with that stuff in a long time."

"And why is that?" I asked.

"Christians don't like being around me. They can't handle it. They can't handle me." His voice sounded hurt, like it had been run over a few times, as he continued, "And every time I'm around them, I feel worse than I did before. All they do is tell me about how I'm screwing up, how I'm not measuring up. It just makes me feel worse. I feel bad enough about some of the things I've done already. I'm not proud of a lot of them and those things are with me all the time. I don't need them throwing fuel on the fire."

"That sucks, man. I'm so, so sorry," I said.

"No, dude. It's okay . . . I don't know." Matt started playing with his napkin. "But if the way they treat me is the way God does, then I guess he doesn't want me around either. Maybe that's why I'm not into Jesus. Maybe I'm not convinced he's okay with me. You know?"

"Yeah. I do."

It was sad to see him like that after all these years, and I don't mean sad as in pathetic. He's not pathetic. I mean sad as in I wanted to weep for him. It was truly sad to see what the Stampede has done to him.

Matt still believes that his mistakes have tainted him, that he'll never be good enough for most of the Christians in his life, or for God either. In his mind, it's like he's not even Matt. It's like he has a new name. In his mind, he's now Foolish. In his mind, he is his sin. But for Matt, and for Tyson, and for everyone who's been crushed with guilt and shame, there's hope, because if judgment tramples a soul and tears it apart, grace is the thread capable of stitching it back together.

Real grace, God's kind of grace, opens the door to excessive healing and is fierce enough to handle any and all sin. In grace, shame and guilt evaporate and we are liberated from the burden of performance. In grace, honesty and openness are possible. In grace, we are accepted. In grace, we are not our mistakes and we can be led into truth.

As a generation, that's what we need from people. That's what we need to give each other. Grace. And sure, if we offer grace, that doesn't guarantee that restoration will happen, but without the offer, we guarantee that it won't. And no one in my life has shown me grace's magnificent potential for healing quite like my friend Dale. He showed me grace in an area of my life where I had lost hope that I could ever find it.

Let me explain.

As Gracious as the Stars

People are drawn to Dale like motorcycle enthusiasts to Sturgis, and I totally understand why. Few people are as welcoming as he is, and it's not in a creepy game-show-host kind of way, but in a way that is real and soft, in a way that you can believe. If Dale were an animal, he'd be a koala bear, I think. Against the backdrop of the Rocky Mountains, we met and, over time, became friends with a long list of memorable moments. But all others pale compared to the night we sat in my Jeep beneath the star-coated sky.

My heart was heavy that night.

I should probably put the top up. It's chilly out tonight. No, I can't. I need to have it down. Tonight I need the sky. I need to be able to see it when I stare up, because tonight I want to be open, and this divine big top frees me to do that.

I don't know why. I guess I trust the stars. They are my uneasily offended friends.

In those days, similar to a guy who goes to an all-you-can-eat rib joint in sweat pants so as not to be limited by a belt, I refrained from exclusive dating relationships so that I could take all I could from a broader assortment of the opposite sex. Drifting from girl to girl, sometimes knowing her name and other times not, I would take what I wanted physically and then move along. The next woman wasn't always one made of flesh and blood; sometimes it was a static Internet image or steamy HBO seductress. Real girl. Porn star. Porn amateur. Whichever was fine with me, and over the years I hopped onto the sexual merry-go-round lifestyle more and more, until it eventually became my dictator.

It was a weekly if not nightly ritual for me, spinning me in empty and painful circles, up and down, around and around. As it ruled me, the guilt and shame piled on, and I continued to disappear.

I'd sit on the floor. I'd put on my socks, first right and then left, and as I did, I'd hear that unspeakably rancid voice.

I'm no longer Josh. Josh has vanished. He's gone, rubbed out. I have a new face now. One I don't want to have or look at, one I don't want anyone else to see. I'm now Impure.

Hi, my name is Impure.

At least that's how I saw it. I believed I was nothing more than the sum of my sins, and my mistakes were too much for grace to overcome, and that was more than I could bear.

There were days when all I wanted to do was sleep. It became my sanctuary. If I moved to a different state, I was still there. If I changed the way I dressed or changed jobs, I was still there. But sleep snuck me away from myself, and that felt good, certainly better than what I felt while I was awake. Fearing the judgment of Christianity and God, I ran from those who knew about my ways and refused to open up about them to those who didn't. I was so afraid of being trampled, so afraid of letting anyone see my dirt.

Once, with a group of friends, I tried, but their response was only laughter and below-the-belt mockery. More rejection. My sin was their humor, and I was the punch line.

Walking away from that event feeling so unworthy of their friendship, God, and just about everything else, my heart ached. But I simply kept my womanizing ways to myself and continued. And though I would just as soon keep my dirt in the shadows forever, my life of hiding was no life at all.

Like Tyson and Matt, I just wanted someone to accept me. I wanted so badly for someone to take me as I was, and the bold demonstrations of grace that I had seen in Dale over and over again provided a glimmer of hope that he might be that someone. After all, I had seen him gaze beyond the lies and hate of others and into wounded hearts, past the muddiness of selfishness and pride and into aching spirits. And I wish I could tell you specific examples of how and when I saw that, but I can't.

For some reason, my memory[2] can't re-create those moments, words, and images. I can only clearly remember that he was that way with everyone. All the time. I only remember that wherever Dale went, grace went with him. Unlike most people, he didn't ask others to get themselves together before he accepted them. Dale was willing to talk and walk alongside them regardless of if they got things together or not, and that night I longed for him to do likewise with me.

That's when I told him.

"I did it again. This time with a different girl."

Propped against the grainy steering wheel and staring out through the cracked windshield, I wondered how the next moments would unfold. I have to think that the young man in Christ's parable of the Lost Son wondered something similar on his long journey home.

Seeing beyond the Dirt

I'm on my way back.

I've got no choice.

I tried to make it all better on my own, to get it all back, to make it right again, but I couldn't. No matter what I did, things seemed to just get worse, and now it's gone, all of it. Has been for about a month. I've lost everything that he gave me, and then some. I've lost more than money, more than things, more than an inheritance. I've lost hope. I've lost peace. I've lost dignity.

I've lost myself.

And I'm so hungry. The last time I ate, the weather was much warmer, and the leaves were a different color. Of course, even if someone gave me food, I don't know if I'd have the energy to eat it. Each step takes every last ounce of what I've got, and that's not much. God, I smell awful, and I look worse than I smell. I'm so ashamed of what I've become.

Sigh.

There it is. This is my last chance to turn back. As soon as I come up over this hill, I'll see home, or what used to be home, anyway.

I wonder what my dad will say. I wonder what he'll do. Will he accept me after all that I've done? With all these things that I've done? Will he even see me anymore?

I don't know. I just don't know . . . Daddy. Daddy.

Please, let me call you my daddy again . . .

The younger son, covered in filth, drags his bloodied feet through the front wooden gate, so exhausted that he neglects to latch it behind him. His clothing, regal and impressive the day he left, is now a pile of tattered rags. The stench of pig and vomit hangs in the air around him. Formerly strong and impressive in stature, he is a shell of his former self, with cheekbones now poking through his skin and his legs appearing as though they are one stern breeze away from snapping at the kneecap.

The father is standing in the doorway, watching. Longing. He's been standing there awaiting his kid's return for a long time, so long that his knees hurt.

As the son comes over the hill and enters the gate, the father sees what is left of him, but as he runs out to embrace him, he also sees something that most of us do not see. He doesn't see the labels that so many others have attached to his son. He doesn't see a great disappointment. He doesn't just see the dirt.

He still sees his son.

Running off the creaky front porch, with his son crumbling into a heap, the father takes him by the shoulders, swiftly pulls him into his bosom, and with tears of joy embraces him. Ignoring the foul stench and the slew of questions that he could ask, like, "Where have you been?!" and "What the hell were you thinking?!" he continues holding him and stroking his crusty, unwashed hair, whispering, "Son, I'm still here. Daddy's here. It is so great to see you again."

Thinking about this is overwhelming to me, and I totally mean that.

It's really difficult for me to understand this because in my mind, like everything else, grace has to have a stopping point. A wall. An end. A boundary. But the kind of grace I see here and throughout Scripture doesn't. I don't see a bottom in the grace given to the thief on the cross or the grace given to the mercenary-turned-missionary, Apostle Paul. I don't see a limit to that grace, and that is such a relief, because if there were a limit, there'd be no hope.

There would be no hope for pedophiles and KKK members, no hope for abusive husbands and cheating spouses, no hope for betrayers and liars, no hope for David and Moses, no hope for bad mothers and selfish pricks, no hope for Adolf Hitler and Saddam Hussein, and no hope for me. Deep within my heart I know that I am capable of awful things, of things that I don't want to acknowledge or face. I know that I am capable of great evil. From time to time I actually frighten myself. There are undead ghouls and grizzly henchmen that roam the plains of my mind, moaning and wailing, beckoning me to give in to hate, infidelity, cruel judgment, abuse, lies, indifference, greed, and murder. And I know that because I am a sinner there is always the possibility that at any point, I just may. So without this kind of limitless grace, there would be no hope, because it's the only kind of grace that is strong enough to welcome all of us, the only kind that is stronger than any sin or failure, the only kind of grace that sees beyond the dirt and creates a context for something divine.

This is the kind of grace that God has for every single one of us, but the question is: Do we have this kind of grace for others? Do I? Do you?

Are you offering limitless, fierce, wall-less, bottomless, "beyond the dirt," overwhelming, liberating, refreshing, tireless, relieving, restoring, restful, celebratory, unoffendable, uncensored grace to those in your life? Am I?

If we want to play a part in the healing of others, we have to pour that kind of grace out. We have to accept people. And we have to accept people again. And we have to accept people again. And we have to accept people again.

And we have to accept people again.

We have to continue to become people who see beyond any and all dirt, not just some of it, and freely give radical grace when others need it most, in the moments when, like the young son, they are filthy.

Mending

Before Dale said a word, his eyes communicated it all, and with a gentle gaze that was both comforting and inviting, and a serenity void of any "What the hell were you thinking?" statements, he opened his mouth and said, "Josh. It's okay."

Seemingly simple and inconsequential words, I know, but when you've repeatedly been told that you're not okay, Dale's response is a dream. After years of my dirt being met with frigid judgment, he saw beyond it. With three simple words, I felt the choking weight of judgment and shame loosed from my neck, the bones broken by the Stampede finally tasting repair, and my sin no longer replacing "Josh" on my nametag. I was accepted.

A tender smile grew over Dale's face as he asked if he could pray for me. Of course I said yes, and in truth, I don't now recall the specifics of what he said, but I can without a doubt tell you the message of that prayer, because it still rings in my heart.

Josh, God loves you more than ever right now. He accepts you no matter how much dirt you have on you and he sees well beyond it. He doesn't boil your entire life down to a few mistakes, a few seconds, a few minutes. God and I will both walk with you toward truth and freedom from this and when you stumble again, grace will be waiting for you every time. We'll both be right here and to us, you'll always be Josh.

Sometimes, it is so difficult to grasp how God interacts with us, until someone gives us a real human illustration of it, which is part of why our lives matter as much as they do. We can be that demonstration for others, just as Dale was for me in that moment. Like God, he embraced me at my worst.

But Tyson and Matt haven't found that yet, at least not as far as I know. So there is no ribbon that I can tie around their stories, no happy ending. We now live miles and states apart, so I don't see them or talk to them very often, but I still think of them often. I want so badly for someone outside the Stampede to show up in their lives—a Dale, someone who will show them God's unrelenting grace, someone willing to embrace them as they are, someone who will help stitch their torn hearts back together, someone, hopefully, like you.

Where the Wild One Is

*Because If God Is in the Worst Places on
Earth, Shouldn't I Be There Too?*

She was about my age. At least I think she was. It was hard
to tell in the middle of the commotion. It's not every day
that a woman runs in front of your moving car, frantically
screaming for help.

Coming to an abrupt stop, I asked how I could help. Without saying a word, she sprinted around the front of my car,
leapt into the passenger seat of my 1997 white Jetta,[1] and
sternly instructed me to drive north. "Now."

Is someone chasing this woman?

I've seen the oft-recurring Hollywood plot where the psychotic ax-wielding boyfriend hunts the panicked girl, leaving
her only hope of escape in the chances of stopping a stranger
and pleading for help. But glancing in my rearview mirror
and seeing no boyfriend and no ax, I moved to alternative
possibilities.

*Is she sick? Is she crazy? Maybe the psychotic boyfriend is
hiding in the bushes!? I think I see something moving behind
the hedges!*

The options were endless. But moved by the urgency in her voice, I stopped wading through all the possibilities and instead pressed the accelerator. Within moments, I found myself driving north with a complete stranger.

She wore white pants; at least they used to be white. A few days' worth of dust and dirt sprinklings now made them more like sand. Her shirt, thin and black, gripped tightly around her shoulders and hung loosely near her neck. Her face was surprisingly soft, and her candy-blue eyes reminded me of the Caribbean Sea.

Passing exit signs at a rate quicker than I could read them, she calmed and we engaged in small talk.

"So what's your name, honey?"

"Josh," I said.

"Well, Josh, thanks so much for picking me up. I just needed to get out of there and I don't have a car. Life can be hard sometimes, you know?"

"Yeah, I think I do . . ."

It was quite pleasant, for a while.

Then, as if Dr. Jekyll mutated into Mr. Hyde before my very eyes, she began screaming at me. High-pitched profanities and insults reverberated off the windows as her voice pierced what was an already tense air. In a vulgarity-laced tirade, I heard how stupid I was, how I didn't know where I was going, and how I needed to drive not north, but south. My brain spun out of control and I arrived at a grim possibility.

What if this woman is luring me to a dark place? To a place where I'll be mugged? Or jumped? Maybe I'll be attacked. Or worse. Worse! Wor—

I can't breathe.

Water is filling my lungs. I'm sinking, drowning in a glass of warm water, trying in vain to swim in a three-piece denim suit. Everything is about to turn black . . .

I felt helpless. Terrified and nearing hysterics, I attempted to figure a way out of my current situation.

Okay, I could slam on the brakes as hard as possible. I've got my seatbelt on. She doesn't! She'll knock herself unconscious on the dashboard. That's it! If Bruce Willis can do it, then so can I . . . No. There's no way that will work. Nothing is going to work. I've got to do what she says.

And I did. Unable to conjure any better options, I submitted to her request and drove south, thinking that when the opportunity presented itself, I would dart off the highway.

And I did just that, sort of.

After turning around and traveling south for a few minutes, I slowly began exiting the highway when my passenger, who had reverted back into the non-volatile, pleasant mode of the previous moments, now began screaming at me yet again, this time threatening me with physical violence.

"I'll kill you! I'll hurt you so bad!" Her voice rang with a spoiled malevolence. "You better do what I say!"

As I continued onto the exit ramp, she reared back and hit me as hard as she could across my right shoulder. Then she hit me again at my elbow and again where the neck meets the collarbone. Each closed-fist wallop hurt more than the one prior. With thumps raining down, she crackled and shrieked for me to pull back onto the highway, and as she did, I became more and more afraid.

Meanwhile, all reason and consciousness within me barked, *Surely God doesn't want this to happen. There's no way he wants me to be in this situation, at this place and at this time. He loves me too much. He loves me, this I know. The parts of his Book that make me feel good, and my fear, tell me so.*

There's no way God would ask me to love this woman. Right?

With heart and mind galloping, those thoughts acted like a balm to raw sunburn. It was soothing to think that God would never put me in harm's way or call me into a situation of fright—

And at this point I'm going to close the curtain on my story for just a moment.

I'm sorry. I hate to do this, but I feel I need to. I promise I'll come back to it and tell you what happened, but after this brief intermission.

Just consider this the end of Act I.

A Maggot to Roadkill

As I said, it's soothing to think that God would never call me into something scary.

Like a warm blanket and a cup of hot chocolate on a cold night, it's comforting for me to think that God wants to keep me away from danger and risk, and asks only that I be a good person, slip into a pew on Sunday morning with some regularity, and chase the American Dream. It's like I imagine God to be tame and domesticated, a conservative spirit who loves nothing more than to drive his wood-paneled station wagon with the radio dialed to easy listening, and I know exactly why. If that's God, then I have permission and maybe even an obligation to chase something I crave.

Comfort. It truly is one of my greatest addictions.

I am, like a maggot to roadkill, drawn to the things that I can handle and the things that I know: the safe bet, the person whose life is stable, the nicer neighborhood, the nonconfrontational conversation, the proven idea, the higher-paying job, safety, and a certainty about what tomorrow will bring. I want to live comfortably, in a thick-cushioned-couch state of being. I want my life to be easy, and I often find myself doing whatever I can to make it so. On some level, most of us tend to operate within this framework. Heck, even Jesus's disciples did.

One of the first Bible stories I ever read was the story of Peter and Jesus walking on water. I love that story. It's part romance, part mystery, part suspense, and part horror film. And it's told in a way that tickles all the senses.

On an angry, stormy night, the twelve disciples are passing over the lake, when they eye a figure approaching on the water. The figure climbs the waves, sneering at the wind. All frightened, only Peter speaks up, and when he does, he asks the figure to prove that he is, in fact, Jesus. When Peter has enough evidence to believe that it is his Rabbi, he climbs out of the boat and walks toward him.

It's amazing, if you really stop and think about it. Peter actually does it! He walks on water. But, like we all know, it doesn't last very long. A few minutes later, Peter begins sinking, drowning in the unforgiving waters, and we often blame this undesirable development on the fact that Peter takes his eyes off Christ. He looks at the obstacles. The waves. The rushing wind. The worst-case scenario. The fear. And because of that, he sinks.

For a long time, this didn't make sense to me, but it does now, and I see the truth in it. When I stare at my fears and worries instead of my God, it seems that sinking and the sensation of being overwhelmed are unavoidable; but I have to tell you, most of the time, in looking so closely at this moment in the story, I miss something else that is even more important.

I'm not like Peter.

Peter was willing to go with Jesus wherever he went, whenever he went. He went with Jesus into the most precarious of situations, even onto the raging water. Peter was willing to try to walk on water to be with Jesus. Peter's life and his relationship with Christ weren't based on convenience. They were based on faith, and when I consider my own life, I have a hard time finding much of Peter in myself.

What I do find, though, is a lot of the other eleven disciples.

While Peter was with Jesus on the waves, they were clinging to the secure wooden vessel below them. They were hiding from faith, and if I were there, that's where I would have been too. Hiding. In that moment, the other eleven disciples didn't want faith. They didn't choose faith. They only wanted one thing. Comfort. Safety. So when the opportunity to live in faith and walk with Jesus into the storm, into the horror film, presented itself, they politely said, "No thanks, I'll stay right where I am." They exchanged faith for comfort, and as that woman hit me and screamed, it's the exact exchange that I wanted to make.

Now, back to the second part of my story.

The maestro raises his baton, and with a flick of his wrist, the overture begins and the lights dim. Finely dressed ladies, and men in tuxedos with expensive cuff links, hustle back to their seats. Intermission is over.

Intermission Over, Begin Act II, Back on the Highway

EXT. Texas Highway—Evening

A white Volkswagen Jetta idles at a stoplight on a busy highway exit ramp.

A WOMAN WITH CANDY-BLUE EYES AND FORMERLY WHITE PANTS sits in the passenger seat. She is not wearing a seat belt. She continues hitting JOSH on the right side of his body. She hits his arm and shoulder. She is shouting and her eyes are flared wide.

We see fear in Josh's eyes. He's on the verge of panic and has an expression suggesting he'd rather be anywhere other than where he is. He wants nothing more than to be in a place of comfort and safety, far away from this woman and away from this situation.

We see his expression now begin to slightly change, from total fear to concentration.

He faintly senses God telling him to stay with her. He knows that it sounds crazy, and maybe it is, but Josh believes that sometimes God's voice is more haunting than inviting. This is one of those moments for Josh. He feels as though God wants him to love this woman in any way that he can.

Josh reluctantly veers back onto the highway, and as he does, he prays to himself.

JOSH (*Whispering*)

> God, I'm so scared and I really need your help, and I need it now. Please, God. Please, God. Oh God . . .

Josh sucks in his lower lip. He now knows what he needs to do. Sure, he isn't the guy who chalks up every strange occurrence to the supernatural. He doesn't believe in UFOs, ghosts, the Loch Ness Monster, or that Elvis is still alive. And while he believes in angels and demons, he also believes in the human imagination.

We see the white Volkswagen Jetta speeding sixty-five miles an hour. The woman with the candy-blue eyes and the formerly white pants continues shouting the most toxic of words. They echo off the windows. She is uncontrollable. Frantic. She seems dangerous.

JOSH (*Taking a deep breath and slowly turning toward the woman*)

> Who am I talking to right now?

113

Immediately the woman goes silent. Her arms stop swinging. She hardly moves a muscle.

JOSH (*Apprehensively, but trying to sound confident*)
> I don't know who I'm talking to, but I want to talk to you!

Again, silence. No response from the woman.

JOSH (*Still nervous, but determined*)
> Do you know who God is?

We see the woman shake her head no. Her eyes are closed and she is facing straight ahead, almost like she is trying to break free from a trance.

JOSH (*Now strong in voice and expression*)
> Well, I know who God is. God's name is Jesus and I want you to know that even though you've been hurt, mistreated, and rejected your whole life, Jesus loves you and he wants to be with you.

We see the woman begin to shake and pound the dashboard. Louder than before. Harder than before.

It is a wild scene.

Josh is careening down the highway, unsure if he is casting out a demon or talking to an addict, but either way, nervous that she is about to launch vomit all over his face like Linda Blair in *The Exorcist*.

CANDY-BLUE-EYED WOMAN (*Screaming loudly and violently*)

Ahhhhh! I'm going to kill you! You have no idea
what I can do to you! Let me out of here!!

She shakes like a Tasmanian devil.

Josh decides that their time together has come to an end.
He pulls the white Volkswagen Jetta off the highway and
into a gas station. He demands she get out of the car, and
she does.

We see her walk away. As she does, Josh exhales deeply
and we sense relief in his body language.

They never see each other again.

(FADE TO BLACK)

God Hasn't Lost His Edge

As I drove home, shaken, the notion that I was just the target
of an evil attack, or that God wanted me anywhere but there,
began to disappear, and it was replaced by an even more unsettling suggestion that began to crop up within my soul.

*Maybe I was supposed to be there. Maybe God wanted
me there. Maybe he loves her too much. Maybe he loves her
too much to not send someone to her.*

With afternoon fading into evening, I began to consider
that God, like some sort of twisted matchmaker or mad scien-
tist, wanted me to encounter that strange woman. And beyond
that, I began to consider that maybe God desires and invites
all of us to those kinds of faith-dependent moments.

Like I said, it's an unsettling idea. I don't like it. But is it
really that far-fetched? If I consider the God of Scripture, the
answer is probably no.

After all, that God sent a boy to fight a ruthless giant
who was ready to tear him limb from limb, and a man to
randomly build a giant boat called an ark. He pitted young,

115

inexperienced followers against petrifying demonic forces and encouraged others to leave all that they had. He asked a young virgin to face accusations and public humiliation and, oh yeah, he later sent his own child into the desert where Satan himself was waiting.

These aren't the actions of a domestic God. These are the actions of a wild and edgy God, and that God freaks me out. That God is unsettling to me. But it's even further unsettling to consider that though it's been thousands of years since the events of Scripture, maybe God hasn't lost his edge. Maybe he still doesn't much care about my comfort. Maybe, instead, God still invites me to become a person of wild faith.

To quit jobs. To sell houses. To move into bad neighborhoods and dangerous countries. To pray big. To give what I feel I don't have. To reach. To dream. To risk. To do something that seems crazy to everyone else.

I love saying that God is the same yesterday, today, and forever, but what I really mean when I say that is, "The parts of God that I like and seem to work to my advantage are the same yesterday, today, and forever." Those parts of God don't change. There are other parts of God, parts that I'm not sure how to handle, parts that, on the surface, don't work to my advantage, parts that I consider exceptions. I think I want this unsettling part of God to be one of those exceptions. I think I want this part to be different now. But maybe it's time that I, and all of us, accept that God is still a wild God, accept that God hasn't lost his edge . . . and accept that maybe it's his followers who have.

Have you?

Sometimes, to evolve into a more powerful agent of change, my heart doesn't need an injection of more church, prayer, or friendship. Sometimes my heart needs an injection of wildness, of edgy faith. Sometimes my heart needs to grow in its belief in an edgy God and move out of comfort and onto the water, or the highway, with him. And sometimes, it's only when I'm willing to do that, that I, or anyone, can bring healing to others.

Scary Mike

Let me tell you about Mike.

Mike is a friend of mine. In recent years our friendship has been damaged, and a good deal of that is my fault. It's not all my fault, but some of it definitely is, so I'm trying to repair it. I'm not totally sure how to do that, but I'm trying, because my fault or not, I love Mike. I care about him a great deal.

If you should run into him at a Christmas party, sit down and don't leave his side. If you stay, you'll hear some of the most interesting stories that you've ever heard. The thing is, most of his stories are pretty racy. One of them culminates with someone pointing a gun in his face and another concludes with Mike exiting a sultry brothel after having unprotected sex with a prostitute. So if you can't handle that kind of content, don't bother.

I guess you could say that his life is frightening. It's frightening to me, and it only became scarier when he went to prison.

An impending drug deal turned police sting landed him there. Standing in a Dallas gas station, preparing to make a substance drop, Mike was rushed by a pack of officers and handcuffed. Then following the court decision, that enough was enough, Mike was forced to call a small iron cell his home for the next twelve months.

I've never been to prison, but it's a scary place from what I understand, filled with violence and caked with the aroma of emotional and spiritual death. I once heard someone label prison the worst place on earth, and it very well may be, but even the worst place on earth wasn't enough to keep my friend Thomas from loving Mike.

Thomas is one of my best friends. He loves fishing, snow-mobiling, and shotguns, and he smells like a lumberjack. Pine and sap mixed with dirt. He would do anything for just about anyone, and that includes Mike.

They've been friends for a long time, and when Mike went to prison, Thomas chose to be an even better friend. He chose to love him even more. He would consistently take time out of his day to go visit Mike. He'd walk through the metal detectors. He'd sit down on a hard plastic stool, and through a cloudy sheet of thick glass, he'd visit with Mike.

When I look at Thomas, I see Jesus.

I don't think Jesus gets enough credit for his courage, though he may be the most courageous person to ever live. He stood among the scariest people in the scariest places. And he loved. That's why Thomas reminds me so much of him.

When I see Thomas, I see courage that makes love possible. In Thomas, I see a wild faith that resembles Jesus, that God is using powerfully in the life of another person. Through Thomas, Mike is finding that even in the worst place on earth, God is with him, that God will always be with him, and he's finding that sometimes healing can be found in the places where we expect only pain.

Our world needs more people like that, like Jesus and like Thomas, because there are plenty of us that are like Mike. As a generation, we are sometimes violent and dark, drugged and angry, depressed and spiritually oppressed. We can be scary people, not for the timid of heart.

So if people won't leave comfort and walk the wild side of restoration, as Thomas does and as Jesus did, others will forever go unreached, unloved, and unhealed. Certain people will never know that John 3:16 applies to them too. Let me put it another way.

By refusing to do what is uncomfortable, we turn our backs on those who make us uncomfortable, people that need us, people like that woman in the car, people like Mike, and people like Bob too.

Artsy Bob

Sometimes people paint their choices as more noble than they really are. This annoys me.

For example, they say that they're going to the bar to reach out to new people in their community, when in reality, all they're really going to do is get tanked on happy-hour drinks. Or they say that they're hanging out with the hot girl because they want to invite her to church, when in reality, all they want to do is sleep with her. I'm guilty of making myself sound more noble than I really am sometimes too, but I won't do that here. I didn't go that night to tell anyone about Jesus, or to change the world. I went to get a tattoo.[2]

But I guess God had more in mind.

I stepped into Bob's shop, which is a lot like most tattoo shops. Upon entering, your ears are cordially introduced to the purring of tattoo guns and heavy metal music, your nostrils to the levitating scent of sanitizing lotion. Adorning the walls are incredible paintings, pictures, and drawings, many of which I could gaze at for hours.

Chinese dragons in fire reds and cool greens. Brilliantly detailed murals of *The Starry Night* by van Gogh. Intricately scripted letters and words that flow like the tail of a comet. Gorgeous landscapes and skies that feel so real you hardly remember you're indoors.

It's a sight to see, but of course, there are also plenty of images not quite my taste.

Nude women engaging in sex acts with figures of all kinds. Representations celebrating Satan and his vile minions. Alarming acts of torture and murder. Rotting skeletons lustfully clinging to scraps of skin and bone. Offensive and irreverent words and phrases.

Yes, the tattoo shop experience is a unique one, and I don't describe it to you in an attempt to push the envelope or shock you, which would be a waste of time and paper. I describe it because sometimes, unless we understand the extent of one's brokenness and the darkness of one's environment, we can't fully understand the edginess of God and how far his extravagant love reaches.

Bob came around the corner and introduced himself; seeing him, I was a little taken aback. I was expecting someone much younger, not someone with wispy gray hair, someone who wears glasses on the end of his nose, someone I might sit on the front porch with, sipping glasses of homemade lemonade. As it turns out, Bob isn't Gen Y, but he lives and breathes a Gen Y–dominated industry, so I think of him as a symbol of my generation. Regardless of age, he seemed like a great guy and was clearly a talented artist, so I sat down and he went to work on my arm.

With the serenade of a tattoo gun, we began talking. After conversation surrounding the specific meaning of the tattoo, it funneled to Bob's dirty jokes, our families, his divorce, his involvement with South American prostitutes, and eventually to God and Jesus Christ, someone that Bob doesn't know. After two hours and some great dialogue, he finished and I, with my new art, went on my way.

Nearly a year later, while sitting in a Japanese fast food restaurant late one night, I saw Bob again. Not really expecting him to remember me, I approached and said hello.

"You're Josh."

He did remember me.

"Yeah! Bob, I want you to know how much I love the art you did on my arm, and if I ever get the funds together, I'm coming back to you for more."

He thanked me and I sat back down, reflecting on the brief conversation that seemed anything but monumental. A few minutes later, as I neared the bottom of my spicy chicken bowl, Bob came over and sat down with me.

"Josh, it's funny that I would see you here tonight. I've been reading a book lately, and as I've read it, I've been thinking about you."

I fiddled with my chopsticks as he continued, "It's a book about Jesus."

God is gently knocking on Bob's soul. He is pursuing him into a place that many who consider themselves followers of Christ would never go. And he's inviting me, in wild faith, to come with him, out onto the water.

So I now go to Bob's tattoo shop for two reasons. To get more tattoos. And to be a part of Bob's healing. I know now that an edgy God is willing to go to him, to Mike, and to that woman in my car.

I guess the only question is—am I?

The Hamster Flew the Plane

Ever since I've known Eric, he's wanted to fly a plane.

He's one of my best friends. He always has been. Beginning in high school, we played soccer together, traveled together, did stupid things that most teenagers do together, and even did some stupid things that most teenagers don't do together. I won't go into everything, but one night we branded each other with a metal cross in my parents' kitchen. Afterward, mine was infected for nearly a year. It's probably the stupidest thing I've ever done, but it's left me with a great scar and an even greater story, one Eric and I frequently rehash today.

We've been through a lot together, and through it all, he wanted to get his pilot's license, but he never did. In fact, he never even tried. He was always too afraid.

In fairness, I can't say I blame him. I'm terrified of riding a bike. It's that recurring vision of hitting an unexpected bump and taking the handlebars to the crotch that scares me, and I'd prefer not to take that chance, so I stay off. Flying a plane is slightly scarier than that, with potentially much more dramatic ramifications if one crashes. So the fear is somewhat legitimate, and Eric found it legitimate enough to stop him. But this isn't the only area of his life where Eric let fear stand in the way.

He lived in the same town for nearly his whole life, and that's not such a bad thing, I suppose. There is something really sweet about loving an area so much that you willingly remain a part of it forever. But love is not the reason Eric stayed. He, like many, stayed because he was afraid of stepping out of what he knew and into what was uncomfortable.

He didn't date, either, and again, not because he couldn't. As far as the dating universe goes, he has all the necessary attributes to be quite successful. He's good-looking, generous, and has a knack for the funny like few do. But as with flying, he's afraid of this too. Fear has ruled his entire life but sadly, Eric's plight is not unlike many within my generation. We are ruled by fear.

We fear love. We fear community. We fear our dreams. We fear intimacy. We fear overcoming.

In short, we fear what we desire most, the life God has created us to live, and our rebuttal to that fear has often been avoidance.

It's almost like we've taken God's words "Fear not" to mean "Pursue what you do not fear" rather than "Walk in faith in the midst of your fears." We've responded by staying where we're comfortable, and that's exactly why so many of us end up lonely, in lifeless jobs, and distant from our Creator, because all the things we long for most require faith. But what's made avoiding our fear so easy is that it seems so normal.

People staying where it's comfortable are normal. People avoiding their fears are normal. People who don't chase a dream are normal. People who reject intimacy are normal. The eleven disciples in the boat are normal. But people who face their fears, chase a dream, take a risk, people who are willing to live in faith—now that's rare.

Peter is rare. But it's those rare people like Peter who take others out of fear.

It's those rare people who live lives of faith that move others toward faith too. It's those rare people that this world needs, and I'd like to be one of those people, I think. I'd like to be a person that moves others toward the things they long for, toward the things God has created them for, and with God's help, I'm very slowly becoming one.

V . . . e . . . . r . . . y . . . S . . . l . . . . o . . . w . . . . l . . . . y.

Part of what I've had to do in that process is face a fear that grabbed me when I was in the second grade. It all started when Mrs. Landrum, my teacher, gave us an assignment to complete this story:

You are riding on an airplane with your pet hamster resting in his cage underneath your seat. Midway through the flight, you peer under your seat and find that your hamster has escaped! You begin looking for him when . . .

My story concluded with me opening the door to the cockpit and finding my hamster wearing a pilot's cap, flying the plane. My teacher loved it and I, in turn, fell in love with creating stories. But that love was strangled quickly, and as I got older, I wrote less and less frequently. I'm sure that girls and video games were, in part, to blame, but mostly it was, just like with Eric, fear.

I was so afraid of hearing that I was no good, hearing that I didn't know how to string words together in a compelling way, hearing that my imagination and ideas were too weird, so afraid of having my work rejected, that I took the more appealing route. Avoiding it. Not doing it at all. For almost eighteen years, I didn't write, out of fear.

Finally, at the age of twenty-six, I decided to begin facing my fear, so I started writing, a lot.

Journaling. Messages. Articles. Fiction. Nonfiction. Poetry. And even books.

I wrote and wrote and wrote. Some of it was pretty good, and some of it sucked, but nearly all of it, since I was still too cowardly to put it before anyone else's eyes, was kept between me and myself. I guess I felt that both my work and myself were safe there. But a few years later, I faced that fear. I read poetry to trusted friends and began submitting articles to magazines and online publications. Some were published and others laughed at, but regardless, I kept writing, and as I did, I shared my journey with Eric.

He had long known of my desire to write and my fears that came along with it. As I slowly walked in faith into my fear, he saw the disappointments and the breakthroughs, all the while offering nothing but encouragement and support, fueling my efforts. The day that I received news that my first book, this book, was going to be published, I called Eric and we celebrated together. What I didn't know was that as I was facing my fears, in faith, God was stirring something in Eric's own soul to face his. Shortly following our day of celebration, I received this email from Eric.

Yo man, I just wanted to say how happy I am for you. Not because you got this book deal but because you decided to do something that most people don't do. You decided to go out on a limb. You followed a dream that was scary. But you and I both know that your dream, however scary it may be at times, brings more joy than we can fathom. I am so happy that you don't live your life in fear. You live it with faith. Thanks for the example you have set; your writing and lack of fear has helped inspire me. I think of fear every time I get in the cockpit now and how ridiculous it is to live with it. Here's to punching fear in the balls. –Eric

My friend Eric inspires me, and his fears continue to die at the hands of a God who doesn't drive a station wagon. Eric has now earned his pilot's license and is allowing God to take him into the teeth of other fears as well. Though the move toward intimacy was dreadfully uncomfortable, he walked in faith there too, and is now married to an amazing woman.

Oh, and by the way, they're moving to England.

He Came from London

Finding Relevance While Destroying an Evil Empire

At first, I swore that he was a department store mannequin that had come to life. It seemed to be the most logical explanation for his shockingly pale face and nearly transparent blond hair. His wardrobe choice was interesting, to say the least: tight black suit pants topped with a tucked-in, ultra-thin, collared, white shirt, and shiny black snakeskin shoes. I remember him being sweaty, probably because he was ranting and raving, whirling around, and pointing at people as he bellowed Bible verses. Standing in the center of a bustling plaza in downtown London, an evangelist was preaching to a gathering crowd and I was too interested to walk by.

So I stopped and listened as he fired eardrum-bursting phrases that reminded me of so many other bullhorn-toting street preachers.

"The end is near!"

"Repent!"

"If you died tonight . . ."

And so on.

I don't know if there is an intersection evangelist school where these preachers learn all the phrases and motions, but if there is, this guy must have graduated at the head of his class.

He was at the top of his "turn or burn" game. His attention was fixed firmly on his temporary flock, when suddenly he turned toward me.

Walking as briskly as his portly body would allow, he approached, thrust his long spiny index finger in my face, and shouted, "YOUR TATTOOS WILL NOT SAVE YOU FROM HELL!"

He barked, saliva spraying from his mouth.

"YOUR MUSCLES WILL NOT SAVE YOU FROM HELL!"

He got within a few inches of my face, stopped, and stared at me as I stood silently.

Then he spun around and continued, this time in the direction of another plaza visitor. I remained for a few more minutes, saw more of what I had already seen, and left, stopping to see other street performers around the plaza.

A man covered from head to toe in metallic silver paint, standing as still as a statue, who upon receiving a bill or coin in his basket, would change positions suddenly, to the roar of the crowd, and then retire again to his frozen state. A juggler, tossing and catching bowling pins and flaming sticks while resting precariously upon a stretched unicycle. Three children treating buckets as drums, thumping to a city club-like beat, moving the entire crowd to cheers and prompting others to dance spontaneously.

It was all really cool, but with every performer that I watched, enjoyed, and even admired, I couldn't get my mind off the evangelist.

Relevance Is Not a Beard

Jesus. Relevance. Those two words seem to go hand in hand.

Jesus had a knack for the relevant like few others, maybe like none other, and it's always amazed me. He always seemed to be right on target with culture and people of all kinds.

Rich people. Beggars.

Farmers. Slaves. Soldiers. Fishermen. Prostitutes.

Officials. Religious people.

Men. Women. Children.

It didn't matter who it was. Somehow, he was relevant. Some people hated him and some people loved him, but whether they agreed with him or not, everyone listened to him. But when I look at his life and ask, what made Jesus relevant to the world around him? I'm not satisfied with an answer that points to anything external, which, oddly enough, is the very place we seem to think relevance is found.

"O Relevance, Relevance, Wherefore Art Thou Relevance?"

The places we look for relevance and the things we do in order to be relevant

Hairstyles: We change our cut/style in order to look younger or edgier, more with the times

Clothing: We wear T-shirts that say "anarchy" or whatever else is currently in, and maybe some trendy jeans too

Music: We listen to music other than what is really us, just so we can show people that we don't only know and enjoy tunes written pre-1991

Branding: We title sermon series after current television shows

Buildings: We make sure that our churches look like, smell like, and function like malls, theaters, stadiums, and other places that are more mainstream

References: We are good at mentioning things that are reasonably recent—this could be a movie quote, song lyric, a brand name, Starbucks, an actress, a style, or even some slaying term that other people are using nowadays

Fame: We want to be known by everyone through a series of television, film, talk show, stadium, and magazine cover appearances

Those are some of the things we do in order to be relevant to this world, to my generation, and some of them actually help. Sometimes, even the smallest bit of common ground can make all the difference in a relationship; plus, we live in a superficial world, and we can be a superficial generation, so the above do aid relevance. They can take one or two bricks out of someone's wall, but they fall way short and always will, because ultimately, relevance is not an external issue.

It's an internal one.

Jesus wasn't relevant because he wore the latest in tunic and sandal fashion. He wasn't relevant because of his age, the particular way in which he groomed his beard, or simply because he shared interests with the people at large. He is one of the most interesting people of all time, but that's not ultimately what made or still makes him relevant either. Something much further below the surface made and still makes Jesus relevant.

Humility. It may seem strange, but if I could point to one thing that made Jesus relevant to the world, that would be it.

He treated everyone with respect and wanted to know and learn about people of all kinds. He didn't simply have the same interests as someone else; he was always interested *in* that someone else. He spent time among people, with them, and believed people to be beings of infinite depth, gifting, and importance. He served. He asked questions and listened, and because of this way about him, he understood people, why they hurt, their desires, interests, and what they really needed.

I'm sitting in a coffee shop right now, thinking about this very idea.

This particular coffee shop smells like old wooden planks and has red Christmas lights up over the cash register. A picture of Jesus hangs directly next to a painting of a woman in yellow lingerie, and as I see it, I start to imagine this humble Jesus.

I'm writing and sipping my coffee. Bollocks, I should have put more cream in it. Oh my gosh! That's . . . no. It can't be. No, it is! That's Jesus, and he's walking over to me.

You want to sit down with me, Jesus? Absolutely, Jesus. I'd really like that. Wait, you want to know about me? Okay, well, where do I start?

I talk for a while and he's interested, really interested. In me. He asks my opinion and why I believe what I do. He doesn't take his eyes off me. It's like I'm the only person in the room, the most important person in the world to him.

We talk about everything—we even talk about why his picture is hanging in the coffee shop. He isn't bothered that it hangs next to a woman in yellow lingerie. He says that's exactly where he needs to be. He buys me another cup of coffee and brings it back to me. It has cream in it, and it's distributed perfectly. He knew I wanted cream. He doesn't shout or preach at me. He doesn't talk the whole time.

I don't know exactly why; I guess his humility doesn't let him.

As Christians, we seem to be so obsessed with the idea of relevance. WE'VE GOT TO BE RELEVANT. WE'VE GOT TO BE RELEVANT. WE HAVE GOT, GOT, GOT TO BE RELEVANT . . . but maybe we don't need to be. Maybe we don't need to talk about, focus on, or become more relevant. Maybe we need to talk about, focus on, and become more humble and maybe if we did, relevance would take care of itself.

Maybe that's the conversation we need to have. Maybe that's the idea we need to wrestle with. What does it look like for us to live humbly?

I've had the privilege of knowing a person of challenging humility, a person who shed a great deal of light on this conversation, a person whom God used to shake thousands of lives, including my own, to the core. My mom. I'll tell you a little bit about her.

Mom—A Patchwork of Humility

She was born in Philadelphia, the only child of Helena and George Gostovich, with the soul of a palm tree—strong and confident, gentle and lovely, slightly wild, and without the tiniest hint of pretentiousness.

Every time that she chewed gum, she cracked it loudly and incessantly. She was a big fan of James Taylor and her favorite movie was *Tootsie*, starring Dustin Hoffman as a cross-dressing soap opera star. When she watched it she laughed and imitated the scenes. It's fair to say that she wasn't exactly the churchy type. She never played the organ or folded bulletins, and her brand of humor was too crude and sarcastic for most Sunday afternoon potlucks.

I remember when she audibly booed a preacher after he began a sermon illustration with a degrading comment towards women. Then there was the time when, at fifteen years old and still on my learner's permit, I was driving on a busy Chicago highway, and unknowingly swerving between two lanes. Pulling up next to me, a clearly disapproving semi-truck driver rolled down his window and shouted at me, "Hey!! Where the f— did you get your license?!!" My mom, swiftly moving to my fragile, adolescent defense, rolled down her window and shouted back, "He doesn't have it yet!" She was one of a kind.

For the better part of her life, she worked as a high school teacher, and she was great at it. Of course, the only thing she loved more than teaching was learning. It was a passion of hers, so she read everything she could get her hands on. At night, after hours of study, she oftentimes fell asleep half submerged under books in process of being marked up by pens and highlighters. She believed she could learn from anything and, especially, from anyone.

As a kid and even as I got older, she introduced me to all kinds of people and cultures. She took me to a Buddhist temple, a Baha'i temple, and to a Jewish synagogue, and introduced me to Benny, her gay friend, and Thelma, her striking African-American friend. Each time she took me somewhere, she reminded me to be respectful, and that I was there to learn about them, listen to them, and serve them. She loved listening to people and their stories. More than telling her own.

She . . .

> . . . celebrated the work, ideas, and creativity of others.

> . . . gravitated towards the down and out, those in the margins, the rejected. Part of the reason for that, I think, is because that's how she saw herself, as a little bit of an outsider.

> . . . understood that she had her own junk too.

. . . asked great questions.

. . . was open to new things and ideas, and she loved diversity.

. . . could admit when she was wrong, because her focus was always on the other person, and not on being right.

. . . believed that people were worth knowing and treated others in such a way that they felt spectacular. Important.

. . . asked people what they needed, and then tried her best to meet that need.

. . . took the time to both discover and understand people's interests, hurts, and needs and because of that, regardless of the at times decade's difference in age and style, she was as relevant to others as anyone, and because of that, lives changed.

People wanted to be around her, so they pursued her, and let her in. When students wanted answers, an opinion, or guidance, they came to her, not the younger, cooler, or more externally relevant teacher, and when they did, she could speak tough truths to them. Her words mattered to them. Well into their thirties, former students, along with fellow faculty members, would come to her, write her, and find her for direction, and she offered it to them, all the while continuing her quest to know them, instead of just speculating.

People were with my mom the same way people were with Christ, and I don't think that's just my "momma's boy" bias talking. Her humility is what made her relevant and because of it God used her in inspiring ways. If only there were more like her; if only more hearts beat with that kind of humility. If only mine did.

If only I wasn't so much like that street evangelist.

Empire of the Arrogant

Strolling through that London plaza, I continued thinking about him.

While his approach was blunt and abrasive, and I certainly didn't align myself with all that he said, much of it I actually agreed with and believed to be true. In fact, much of what he said that entire gallery probably needed to hear, but I knew his message wouldn't be received. It wasn't going to last, live on, or bring any kind of healing, because he was irrelevant.

That part I knew. What I didn't know was why. I couldn't put my finger on why he was irrelevant. So I kept thinking about it.

Maybe he's irrelevant because he won't stop shouting, and spitting as he does. Or maybe he's irrelevant because of his skin-tight pants and shirt so thin I can see his nipples. Oh gosh, I saw his nipples!

Shudder.

Well, that certainly doesn't help, but I don't think that's why.

In the same way that something external doesn't ultimately make us relevant, something external doesn't ultimately make us irrelevant either. I kept thinking.

Maybe he's irrelevant just because he's a street evangelist. I've never personally known a relevant street evangelist. Maybe all street evangelists are irrelevant and that's just the way it is.

But as I drilled down further and further, I exhumed something else. I recognized that what really made him irrelevant was how he treated me.

Around him, I felt like a worm, like I didn't matter, like a lowly pawn to his king. I felt unimportant, like I wasn't worth knowing, like there was nothing of value in me, like I could be fully understood, inside and out, with a simple glance. He thought he knew everything about me, as if my past, my soul, and my mind were his childhood bedroom. He was certain he knew what I thought, how I lived, what I wanted, and what I needed. But he didn't. He didn't know the questions I was asking about God, my struggles, and my fears, so while he was talking to me, he wasn't speaking to me. He didn't know anything about me, and he didn't care to find out. What made him irrelevant was his arrogance.

In retrospect, I should have recognized it earlier. The same trait made me irrelevant too.

I used to think that under no circumstances could I possibly be irrelevant to my generation. After all, I was young. I had tattoos, earrings, and in my opinion, an average sense of what was cool. I used to think that way, but I don't anymore, thanks to Eddie.

He had tomato-colored hair and a deep love for science fiction movies, and he wrestled to work out his aggressions on life. I, on the other hand, though I may be a nerd at heart, draw a line just short of reveling in the world of sci-fi. I won't let myself go there. I can't let myself go there. I'm too afraid that if I do, I'll wake up one day, years from now, speaking Elvish to my new friends at a Star Trek convention. So that was a similarity Eddie and I weren't going to share, and unfortunately, wrestling wasn't a common point for us either. At the time, I was still a little creeped out by the whole wrestling thing. I don't know, maybe it was the tight uniforms and the white thighs. Regardless, it just wasn't my bag.

So Eddie and I definitely had our fill of differences, lots of them, but I still thought I knew and understood him pretty well.

From my "enlightened" perspective, he was an angry man; frustrated with the way his life had turned out thus far and pissed at his dad for leaving him and his mom high and dry while he was a kid. The social scene wasn't really his bag, and when he was forcibly thrust into it, he remained in the corner like a musty cobweb. As far as God went, he didn't even show up on Eddie's radar. He was a complete and total afterthought. Yeah, I believed I knew Eddie. I was convinced that I had him nailed, that I was finely tuned to what he needed.

So I told him. I guided him. I offered my wisdom and what I thought he needed, but predictably, Eddie didn't care about what I thought or what I said. He wasn't interested in my ideas or in me, and was instead icy and unresponsive, and now I know why. The reason is pretty simple.

In Eddie's eyes, I was just like that street evangelist. In fact, I might as well have thrown on the shiny, snakeskin shoes, stood out on the street corner, and shouted at him in a thick, British accent. To Eddie, the street evangelist and I were the same. And the truth is, he was right.

I wasn't interested in Eddie or in getting to know him. I didn't care about what he thought, why he thought it, or what was really going on in his heart. I wasn't in Eddie's life to serve him, but instead to do whatever I wanted to do. My actions toward Eddie revealed my heart to Eddie—I believed I was better than him, more important, and while he wasn't worthy of being served, I was. I was most interested in my opinions, my beliefs, my answers, my ideas, my agendas, and myself, and it goes without saying that this is completely contrary to the way Jesus lived. We already talked about that.

But this is also contrary to the way Paul encourages the church to live.

Words Like Trains and Something So Oddly Powerful

Sometimes I read the Bible. And sometimes I don't. That's not a point of pride for me, just the opposite actually. Call it laziness. Call it apathy. Call it unfaithfulness. I suppose my reasons for not engaging it more are a little bit of each, but there's more to it than that. There's also a part of me that, at times, flat out wants to avoid the Bible. Don't get me wrong, I believe in it very much, that there is nothing else in this universe like it, that it is perfect, that it breathes, that it is the Word of God, and yet sometimes I want to distance myself from it. My primary reason is I know that the Bible possesses the potential to cut me, to get into me, to bowl me over with conviction.

There are instances when as soon as I open it, I hear the conviction coming towards me, like a train, cruising down the tracks. I know that if I linger for too long, bells ringing, gates descending, black smoke gathering, I'm going to get hit. I know that if I honestly read certain passages, I'll be certain that the words pertain to me, that I need to hear them, that I'm the target audience. The Apostle Paul has some words like that.

He said, "Do nothing out of selfish ambition or vain conceit, but in humility consider others better than yourselves" (Phil. 2:3).

See what I mean? With these words, I hear the train coming . . .

Chugachugachugachuga. Choo! Choo!

Paul is talking to me and I know it. Hearing these words reminds me that humility isn't commonly my way of life, and that's why I want to avoid them, because I don't want to be reminded of my sin, of my pride. And I don't want to think about the ramifications that humble living has. And it has major ramifications. Humble living means more than stooping, more than placing myself on an even plane with others, which is what I often do. It means putting others ABOVE me. It means kneeling, putting myself BELOW people, BELOW others in my generation.

It all sounds so excessive, but that's because it is. When it comes to humility, there is no halfway. Jesus certainly didn't go halfway. He served. He listened. He gave. He was interested. It seems that he treated people not as equals, but as superiors; as if they were more important than him, more valuable than him. That's excessive, and that's the point. That's exactly what makes humility so oddly powerful, such an unexpected and unusual force of change. That's why humility overcomes differences in age, style, and taste. That's why humility is the source of relevance.

Consider how differently we might interact with people, with each other, with this generation—and the kind of change that might emerge—if we were to embody this kind of excessive and oddly powerful humility.

Perhaps then we might move further into this generation rather than separating ourselves from it, be students of this generation rather than presuming to be the professors of it, and realize that we can learn more from others than they can learn from us, that we need them more than they need us. Perhaps then we wouldn't approach people as projects but rather as human beings, we would see ourselves as servants rather than saviors, be creators instead of imitators, and carry towels rather than checklists. Perhaps then we would ask more questions rather than giving more answers, listen to stories rather than only telling our own, and wrestle with how to meet their needs instead of asking them to fit in with what we're already doing.

Perhaps then, if we lived with excessive humility, as Christ did and as Paul encourages, we would be the kinds of people that my generation needs. Perhaps then we would realize that the most relevant thing we can ever do for someone is to serve them. And perhaps then change would bleed out from us and into countless lives. I think so.

Of course, if you're like me, you need a little help getting there.

Assisted Kneeling

There are moments when life demands scary prayers, prayers that seem to beg for trouble. One of the scariest prayers that I've ever said came after I encountered my shortage of humility and my surplus of arrogance. I guess I didn't want to pray it as much as I felt that I needed to pray it.

God. I'm arrogant and I know it. I don't want to be, but I am. I think I'm more important. But I want to change. I do. So whatever has to happen for me to become more humble— no, no, no . . . excessively humble—please do it.

Oh man, I hope I don't regret this.

The first time I said that prayer, I was confident that God, as if he had a vendetta against me, was going to teach me one of those awful lessons in the most awful of ways, and that something tragic was going to happen to me or someone I loved. So I waited for the jarring phone call, the pink slip, the car accident, or the wheelchair, but it never happened.

Instead, as I confessed my pride daily, God began slowly changing me. It was like someone removed a burlap sack from my head, because for the first time, my eyes began to see, with sharp clarity, my brokenness, his greatness, and the treasure that is other people. And as that happened, I began digging further into the lives of others, as a servant.

I asked questions, such as, "What do you need?" and "How can I help?" I learned. Not approaching others as if I were the professor, but as the student. Who they were became of interest to me, and I was amazed at how that created more humility in me in an organic sort of way. Simply putting others above myself, listening to them, learning from them, and getting to know them showed me the infinite number of reasons I have to be humble. Over time, the empire of arrogance that had dominated my heart for so long began waving the white flag of surrender and crumbling. I was changed. But I know that change can so easily be undone.

The empire never fully surrenders. It can and will attack at any time. Even on the most peaceful of days, in the most serene of moments, arrogance can invade, crossing into the border of my heart and pillaging everything in sight.

So even now, I utter that same scary prayer, and even now, I brace myself for the tragic to follow soon after. But I'm beginning to think that as I'm willing to be humbled and as I seek to live humbly with others, God doesn't twist his moustache and thumb through the variety of ways that he might make my life miserable. I'm beginning to think that he smiles, knowing that as I become a more humble man, I become a more relevant one too. I think he smiles, knowing that as I become more like him, I become more like the man my generation needs me to be.

Shedding Mannequin Skin

First steps are often some of the hardest. That's why, most of the time, I end up standing still.

My first step with Eddie was no exception. It was a difficult one for me, difficult and humbling. But I did it. I went to one of Eddie's wrestling meets, and immediately I was a fish out of water, a Baptist preacher on the Howard Stern show.

Elephant-gray wrestling mats, athletes, trainers, and ranting coaches covered the gymnasium floor and the whole place smelled like socks. Scanning the overwhelming mob scene, I spotted Eddie's mom, made my way up the creaking wooden bleachers, and took a seat next to her. She looked surprised to see me, which didn't really surprise me at all. As we sat together, I asked questions, and as she spoke, I listened, and I learned. I learned about her intense love for her son, her family, and her struggles at her job. When Eddie wrestled, she came to her feet and screamed, unable to take her eyes off him, and when he won in quick and impressive fashion, she beamed with pride.

Following the meet, I found Eddie and said hello, and over the next few weeks and months, we spent more time together. As we did, I served him as best I knew how. I asked him wrestling questions and science fiction questions, even Star Trek questions. I listened to him talk about his family and his girlfriend. I learned more about him, grew to understand him more, and found that the guy that I thought was Eddie wasn't really Eddie at all. Eddie wasn't angry. He was compassionate and tender. He wasn't averse to the social scene. He was just cautious, and liked observing people. And my perception of Eddie's interest in God? Well, as it turned out, that was way off too. And I mean way off.

One afternoon, at the conclusion of a brief conversation, Eddie said, "Hey, Josh. Could you do something for me?"

"Sure, Eddie."

"Are you sure? Because if it's a problem, it's really okay."

"No, seriously. What is it?" I asked.

"Well, the thing is, I'm not really sure what I believe about God or what I think about the Bible. But I've got a lot of questions about both of them. And I wanted to know if you'd be willing to talk through them with me."

"Absolutely. I'd love to."

A few days later, Eddie and I got together and he came with his written list of questions, over one hundred of them. And

142

starting with number one, we talked through them. God was on Eddie's mind after all, and in ways that I didn't have God on mine. His questions were insightful and challenging, deep and penetrating, so much so that I found myself responding to most of them with, "I don't know, Eddie, what do you think?"

And as he talked, I learned, which was interesting at the time, but now commonplace in my life. I usually learn a lot more about life and Jesus from those who are outside the church, rather than those who are in it. From Eddie, I learned not only about God, faith, and myself, but about Eddie too, and I think that was the best part. I learned about who he was, who he wanted to be, the things he thought about, and what he really needed from me. It was amazing.

Suddenly, I had shed that layer of street evangelist skin. I was no longer the uninterested, portly, checklist-toting mannequin come to life. I was relevant, and Eddie wanted my friendship. He wanted to know my opinion, what I thought and why I thought it. And through that, I was given the chance to care for him, to provide accountability, and best of all, to see Eddie open his life to Christ for the first time. But that privilege didn't become mine because I was scrambling to be relevant; rather, because I was finally willing to be humble. Not because I did anything externally, but because I finally let God do something internally.

What an unexpectedly powerful difference it makes.

Every now and again, I wonder what would have happened if that evangelist had interacted with me humbly, like Jesus, or my mom. I wonder what would have happened if he had walked up to me and said,

"Hey, what's your name?"

"Josh," I would say.

"Great. Josh, am I wrong? Or do I detect an American accent?"

"Yeah," I would say, "that's right."

"Terrific. Well welcome to England. What are you here for?"

"I'm actually here with a group of people," I would reply, "and we're here to serve an elderly home, help clean up a neighborhood, and learn about your culture."

"That is so cool."

Maybe our conversation would wind and turn, and after thirty minutes it would come to an end. But maybe, before we parted ways, he'd say, "Hey, just a thought, Josh. Would you like to get together again tomorrow morning?"

"Sure, that sounds great," I would say.

Maybe we'd get together again the next morning, and maybe he'd continue asking about me. Then maybe, after another hour of conversation, I'd ask him, "Hey, is it okay if I ask you a more personal question?"

"Sure," he'd say.

"Well, there's something about you that, I don't know . . . just seems different. What is it?"

And then maybe he'd tell me about the humble Jesus that he knows, and then I think I'd pause and ask him to tell me more about his God and his own life, because he's not just interested in me being interested in him. He's interested in me. He treats me with importance and value. He wants to know me. He wants to meet my needs.

He's relevant to me, so I want to hear what he has to say.

Artificial Paradise

Freeing Captives of a Plastic Lie

Dylan has been one of my dearest friends for a while, and of the bunch, he's the most opinionated, but I'm kind of fond of that aspect of him, usually. He's passionate about what he thinks and believes, which is far more interesting than where so many fall, apathetic and with no opinions. When he reaches his twilight years, there's really no question that he will be the ornery old man screaming at neighborhood kids to stay out of his azaleas and herb garden. I really hope I'm around to see that.

His parents have one of those Johnny and June relationships, one that you look at and say, "I want what they have." Even now, with Dylan in his twenties, they still take family vacations to northern Michigan with him and his sister. They get along really well. Dylan loves his sister and his family, and lives his life in hopes that others might encounter a similar love. Through him, they are.

He's changing my generation and the world.

But it wasn't always that way.

The Plastic Lie

Dylan hails from a land of privilege, a place with white picket fences, private schooling, and low crime rates. It's a wealthy area, where people get what they want. That's not necessarily bad, except for the fact that what most people want is greatly misguided.

Nicer cars. Bigger homes. Hotter wives. Bulging bank accounts. Success. Accolades. Fame.

In Dylan's hometown, that's the carrot that many spend their lives chasing, and I watched as Dylan began chasing it too. Things crept to the front of his mind and onto the tip of his tongue. He spent much of his waking hours thinking about them and reaching for them. I guess you could say that he became a product of his environment. He didn't necessarily want to, but he did, much the same way that many in my generation have.

Remember those innocent schoolboys in *Lord of the Flies*, who after living on a savage island lose their innocence and become savages? That's us. We've become materialistic, products of our stuff-overload environment. We don't see the glass as half full or half empty—we just want a bigger glass. We are self-indulgent stuff whores, clamoring for it, giving ourselves to it, and gorging ourselves on it.

We are the synthetic revolution, the all-you-can-eat buffet, Santa's red sack, Ebenezer Scrooge, and the gluttons of the meaningless.

For Dylan, he wasn't, like many, after Ferraris and a house in the Hamptons. His desire was for success, respect, and status. Those were the objects of his lust, and though you can't touch them with your fingers, they are every bit as material, and the love and pursuit of them kills the soul just like anything with glitter that sparkles. You'd think we'd know that by now.

That's what we hear from Scripture, from every piece of deathbed wisdom, and from the moral embedded in every episode of *VH1 Behind the Music*. The material doesn't give what we truly want.

Sure, it can offer comfort, fleeting joy, a paper sense of power, laughs, memories, and peace of mind, but it can't offer fulfillment, purpose, a cause, and a reason. Stuff can't offer us a reason to get dressed and set the soles of our shoes one in front of the other day after day. It can't give us a cause to fight through the storms for, or something to die for. It can't speak the language of a soul, and that's why it's so devastating when we spend our life pursuing stuff.

We lose our soul in the process. So even if we get the stuff, we don't ever get what we *really* want.

What we really want, stuff can't provide, and yet, as a generation, we continue chasing it, because we have bought into the Artificial Paradise. We believe that someday, somehow, we'll get enough stuff or the right stuff, and that when we do, the internal void will be filled. But, like we all know, it never is, and instead our quest leaves us cruelly empty, which is exactly where Dylan's quest left him.

He wasn't happy. He wasn't content. He didn't have joy. He was miserable. He was without a purpose, without a cause, and without a passion. He was hollow.

He was, maybe, like two fishermen.

And I'll turn it over to a friend of mine for this next part.

Through the Eyes of a Hermit Crab

This isn't Josh. I'm a hermit crab. No really, I am, claws and everything. I know this is Josh's story, but he wanted me to tell you a part of mine, and I don't get asked very often, so of course I accepted.

I live on the beach, moving from shell to shell and scurrying out of the seawater as it washes onto the shore. Most days, I don't do much except watch.

I watch the faint and fat white clouds as they morph, becoming objects that I love and dream of seeing for myself someday. A pair of whales rolling over the waves becomes a Persian palace becomes three firm oak trees becomes a captain at the wheel of a sturdy sea vessel becomes what I imagine one of those taverns I've heard so much about looks like.

I watch the seagulls. They're so loud and brash, shouting at each other like a bunch of drunken frat boys. They fly over the fish, all kinds of them. I like fish. They are kind and friendly. Affectionate creatures. I don't have to worry about them crushing my shell or trying to eat me, which I like. But I like watching humans most of all, I think. They come here to relax, to play and build castles. Sometimes they find shells and take them home to make them into jewelry. They don't realize that they're stealing someone's house. I know they don't mean any harm by it, but it's still a little rude. They could at least ask, right? But I do like watching them.

The humans I like watching the most are fishermen. We have an unspoken bond. They understand me, I think. Two in particular, Simon and Andrew, are here every day. Well, I should say they used to be here every day. They aren't here anymore. It was the strangest thing.

It was just like any other morning. The wind was tired, barely yawning. They stood there, stinking of brine, like always. They wrapped their calloused hands around thick, rugged nets, and cast them out into the water. As they did, they were talking, like always.

"Simon, I don't know how much longer I can do this," Andrew said.

"I know. I feel the same way," Simon said.
Andrew stared out over the lake. His eyes looked disappointed and discouraged.
"I mean, don't you think there's got to be more to it than this? More to life?"
"Yeah, I do," Simon said, with that same disappointed look.
"I guess, I guess I'm just tired of . . . of . . . of not being inspired. I want that." As Andrew talked, his voice got louder. I could hear him so clearly. "I want to be alive, you know? I want a reason to live, something to really give myself to."
"Yeah, so do I. And we're definitely not finding it in this stuff." Simon sighed and then turned his back to the water.
"Help me pick up this net, would you?"
They didn't know I was there, but I was, and they definitely didn't know that he was there. But he was. I knew. I happen to have tremendous eyesight for a crab. I saw him walking around the bend, but it wasn't the first time I'd seen him. I'd seen him before, so I knew who he was. He came here in the evening sometimes to swim with the kids that snuck out of their houses after dinner. In some ways, he was like a big kid. He'd laugh and throw them out into the water. They always smiled at him. Eventually they'd all gang up on him and try to tackle him, and they would. He let them. There was just something about him that was different. Jesus, that's his name.
He walked up to Simon and Andrew. He must have gotten within ten feet of them before they even noticed he was there. The tide was loud, so they didn't even hear his steps on the sand. Then he shouted to them.
"Come with me and follow me wherever I go, and you'll 'fish' for people from now on!"
That was the weirdest thing I'd ever heard, and I've heard a lot of human conversations. I didn't know you could fish

149

for people, but I guess you can. I leaned out of my shell a little further. It's almost impossible to hear in that thing, and I really wanted to hear what they said in response. But they didn't say anything. Not one word. They just looked at each other and sort of lit up, like the moon does over the water. I hadn't seen that expression on either of them before. They looked . . . alive.

Then, they just dropped their nets and went with him, walking back the way Jesus came. It's almost like he said the magic words. I couldn't believe it. They'd been on my beach fishing every day. That's what they knew. That's what they did. But I guess the idea of fishing for people was more appealing.

I don't know, maybe there's something about humans that needs that. Maybe they need to fish for people, instead of fish, or whatever else. Maybe fishing for fish just isn't enough. Whatever the case, they certainly found what they were looking for in him, and in fishing for people.

A few nights ago, Simon and Andrew came back here. I couldn't sleep. I'd had a grain of sand stuck in my claw for a few days, and it was killing me, keeping me up all night. So I watched them, again, just like the good old days, and just like the good old days, they went to the place they always stood.

"Andrew, can you believe all that's happened since we were here last?"

Andrew didn't answer for a moment. He just looked around, beaming. He waited a minute, like he was just trying to take it all in, and then spoke.

"Honestly? No. Not at all."

"Me neither," Simon said.

"I think the craziest part is what's happened in me, you know?" Andrew said.

150

"Yeah, I do. I totally do." Simon was excited, and he couldn't stop smiling. Then he went on. "I thought that by going with Jesus we'd see some ridiculous stuff. I knew that we'd get to be a part of miracles and lives changing; I guess I just didn't realize that my life would be one of them. I just didn't think about how much my life would change."

"That's exactly what I mean. I didn't realize how . . . what's the word?"

"Filled," Simon interjected.

"Yeah," Andrew said, "how filled I would be. I mean, we fished for all those years and it was fine, but we were so hungry for more. For that sense of purpose."

And now they have it.

Even from my shell, I could see that. I could tell. They weren't the same guys that left that beach. They were different now. They had always talked about wanting a reason, and even I, a hermit crab, could sense that they had it. They had that purpose that they wanted. I guess they just needed to leave the nets and pursue something else in order to find it. I guess they needed to go with Jesus, on his mission, and fish for people.

You know, maybe I should try that. Maybe I should leave this shell and find what I'm looking for.

Holy Pursuit

Can I be honest with you? (This is Josh again, by the way.) I have days when I wake up and I don't feel filled.

My alarm whines and clamors, and in my half-conscious state, I think it's a kid banging a cooking pot with a metal spoon. It's the worst sound in the world, but it doesn't stop, so I wake up, and no matter how warmly the morning greets me, I don't feel satisfied. I slide to the edge of my bed, hesitating and studying the lines on my hands, wondering if there is a reason for me to exist, wondering if I'll be able to again capture the passion that, on many other days, I actually feel. And sitting there, I feel bad, like I shouldn't feel that way, since I know Jesus, and maybe that's true, but the fact remains; sometimes I feel downright empty, like every ounce of innards, emotion, and interest in this world has been stolen out of me in the middle of the night by an invisible man.

Eventually, I get up and walk around my condo, and I see how much stuff I have. I see DVDs that I'll probably never watch again, books that are only days from being placed in a cardboard box and forgotten, shirts that I haven't worn in months, and food that I'm going to throw away before it's ever even eaten. And I always have that moment, that moment when I wonder if the reason I have that empty feeling is because I've got all this stuff, and I wonder if the answer is to simply haul it all out to the dumpster and unload it, all of it. But before I ever actually do, I always pause, think, and conclude that's not the answer.

On those days, and on any day really, I've come to find that the answer to me finding purpose is not just having less or letting go of all my things. I've come to find that the answer is living for more and taking hold of something greater. I've come to find that what I need on those days, when I sit just a little bit longer on the edge of my bed and study my hands, is a renewed vision, a worthwhile challenge. I need to, yet again, in a new way and on a new day, step into and experience what my friend, the hermit crab, saw Simon and Andrew experience.

He saw two men who stepped into a holy pursuit. He saw two men who left stuff to follow Jesus into the lives of others, two men who found purpose, reason, and passion. He watched two men who were changed not just by what they let go of, but also by what they pursued. On those empty days, and on every waking day of my life, I've come to find that's what I need, that holy pursuit, and I think that's what many of us need.

My friends and I need a challenge, a compelling vision for how, with our interests and giftings, we could be used by God to shape lives. We need people like Jesus, people who refuse to leave us in the Artificial Paradise, people who will take us out of a life of stuff and into a life of loving people, because that's where healing waits. But the only people who can do that are those who live the kind of lives that will lead people there, those that live as Jesus did.

All Jesus asked of Simon and Andrew was that they follow him. That has always stood out to me. "Follow me." That's all he says, and implied is that if they follow him, their lives will naturally become about people. Jesus simply invites them to follow him into the life he is already living, so the only way their lives weren't going to be about people is if they stopped following him, and this often gets lost in the translation of my life today.

All too typically, I am as deeply mired in the Artificial Paradise as everyone else, so if people walk with me they're not led into people's lives, but into something equally hollow as the stuff they're already chasing. By following me, the emptiness is simply replaced by another empty thing.

More stuff. Achievements. Success. Morality.

This can't be, not in my life, and not in any of our lives. We have to live the kind of lives that will take the purposeless into a life of purpose, a life that will take them into the lives of others. So the question is, are we? Are you?

Where are you taking others? What are you chasing?

Is your life about fish? or people?

If our lives aren't about people, then we must ask ourselves a tough question: are we really following Jesus?

Sometimes, I just drive. I like to drive. With hills first approaching and then, moments later, becoming specks in my rearview mirror, I feel as though I'm moving through time, like I can visit any age or continent in a matter of seconds with the simple tap of my foot. I don't know why, but that feeling helps me think. It helps me see clearly, sometimes regrettably clearly. Often when I drive, I recognize that my life isn't about people. It's about some*thing* else. I sit in the upholstered quiet and reflect on the hours I spend dwelling on success, new toys, and making more money. I realize that things occupy my mind more than people. I realize how often I ask God for things and how little I pray for him to work in people. And though I hate facing it, I know exactly what that means.

It means that somewhere in the course of my day, week, or year, I stopped following Jesus and started following something else. It means that often Jesus is not my one and only God, but often only one of my many gods. It means that I believe what the Artificial Paradise is telling me. It means that just because I believe in Christ doesn't mean I'm always following him. And there is a difference.

That's not how I want to live out my days. That's not where I want to take others, because healing is not waiting in that place. Not for me, and not for them. I want to follow Jesus into the lives of people and bring others with me, because healing is waiting there.

Even the hermit crab knows that now.

A New Environment

Dylan sat across the dinner table from me. I ate buffalo wings.

I love buffalo wings and always ate them when Dylan and I had dinner. We were together often, but there was a slight difference to the air around us that night. This wasn't just any meal. This one had an ulterior motive, a challenge, and an invitation waiting.

"So, Dylan," I said, wiping blue cheese from my mouth. "I've got an idea for you."

"Okay. What is it?"

"Well, you and I have some friends who are hurting, friends who need someone. You know, someone to love them and walk with them through all the crap. I'm trying to do that with those guys, but they need someone else, and most of the people that we know aren't going to do it because most of these guys are complete jerks. Well, I want you to do it, and this is just my opinion, but I think God wants you to do it too. I think he really wants to use you with them and if you're willing, I believe God will do some amazing things in their lives, and in yours too."

Nice speech, huh? Right up there with Martin Luther King's "I have a dream" and William Wallace's "Freedom" speeches. Okay, not quite. But I sat, curious as to how Dylan would respond.

What's he going to do? I'm asking him to do the opposite of what everyone around him is doing. I'm asking him to chuck the pursuit of his own glory for other people. That's stupid. Who wants to do that? No one does that. Not very often, anyway.

I wasn't exactly brimming with confidence.

When offered a cause to believe in, hordes are still going to choose to live for stuff instead. I know that from doing it myself and watching others do it. But often, because I anticipate people declining, because I assume they are going to reject the offer, I opt to save myself the rejection and not offer it at all, and when I do, even those who *are* willing remain captive.

155

When I hear the crab tell his story about Simon and Andrew, it seems like they were ready. I hear of two guys who were willing to walk off that beach, if someone was simply willing to ask them to walk. All they needed was someone to paint for them a vision of what could be, someone to really challenge them to pursue something greater, someone to say the magic words, and that's exactly what Jesus did. He challenged them to more and that's all they needed.

As it turns out, that's all Dylan needed too.

He accepted, and beginning that night, he began stepping into the lives of his friends and loving them, and in the midst of this new pursuit, he received another challenge.

Chip, the Detroit Lions fan I spoke of in the chapter titled, "The Greatest Show on Earth," had been involved with the AIDS pandemic in Zambia for some years. It was close to his heart and he was looking to bring more people into that cause, people willing to give of their time and resources and go to Zambia, to meet, learn from, and love the people. And he asked Dylan. He invited him to join in that effort, and Chip cast a challenging but inspiring vision for how God might use him to impact lives. The thrust of his message was, "Come with me, and God will use us to weaken the hold that this disease has on a nation and the hold that materialism has on us."

And again, like Simon and Andrew, all Dylan needed was someone to invite him. Chip did, and again, Dylan said yes. That continued a change in him that was so fun for me to watch.

His waking hours were spent raising money and mobilizing others to give financially and of themselves for the sake of a village in Zambia, where people have nothing, not even their health. But this was more than just what he did; it became his cause and as he pursued it, others followed him into it. Both at home and across the world, Dylan followed Jesus into the lives of people, and as he was used to bring healing, his heart kept changing and healing too.

The deterioration of a pervasive emptiness made way for a sense of purpose and fulfillment, a reason to set the soles of his shoes one in front of the other each day. He tasted the things that he really wanted—joy, a mission, and contentment—the things that the Artificial Paradise promised but couldn't deliver.

Which brings us back to the present.

In my friend Dylan, I see a man who buys into the declarations of the Artificial Paradise no more, a man who is following Jesus into the lives of other people, a man of vision, a man being used to bring healing, and a man with purpose and fulfillment. I see a man who's no longer just a product of his environment; I now see a man whose environment is becoming a product of him. And I can think of very few people who I'd rather see others becoming like than my opinionated friend.

Now let's turn our attention to another cul-de-sac in the Artificial Paradise.

A Sad and Popular, Popular and Sad Ballad

My friend Chris has black hair, jet-black.

When he laughs, his head kicks back, and a not-too-loud, not-too-long chuckle floats out of his belly. I consider it the only perfect laugh I've ever heard. It's one of those contagious kinds of laughs, so being around him I can't help but laugh too. I like Chris.

He was raised in an ultra-fundamentalist family that wielded religion like a blunt object, and let's just say it screwed him up. The harshness of his environment led him to believe that there was always something wrong with him; actually, lots of things wrong with him.

He wasn't smart enough. He wasn't handsome enough. He wasn't strong enough. He wasn't talented enough. He wasn't responsible enough. He wasn't hardworking enough. He wasn't quick enough. He wasn't personable enough. He wasn't good enough. He wasn't holy enough.

He became convinced, even at a young age, that he deserved nothing (that seems unnatural to me: a kid thinking that he deserves nothing, not even a hug or an "I'm proud of you, Son"), that he was completely unlovable, worthless, and unworthy of love from anyone, including himself, and that didn't change as he grew older. Actually, it only got worse. His difficulty loving himself slowly morphed into an impossibility of loving himself, and eventually, that became true self-hate. Chris hated himself, and this sad ballad of self-hatred is one that many of us sing.

We hum it. We dance to it. We are swept up in the demented movements, in an unending tango with self-hatred, and it all stems from a lie that makes its home firmly in the Artificial Paradise.

Working in subversive ways, it more often than not goes unnoticed, which is part of why it is so powerful and why it can sink in and slowly destroy someone. The fact that we hear it incessantly aids that too, and boy do we hear it, from everywhere, it seems. Indulge yourself: flip on the TV or walk through the checkout line, and maybe you'll hear it too.

Drop ten pounds! Get bigger arms now! Look younger! Learn what he really wants you to do to him in bed!

That message is pumped to us non-stop, the message that unless we can "look younger" or "do what he really wants in bed," we aren't good enough. And while it may initially strike us as a flaccid attack, it's quite dangerous. It doesn't necessarily work the first time we hear it, or maybe even the second or third time, but eventually, like brainwashing, it does.

After the hundredth or thousandth time we hear it, we begin to believe the lie, and when we do, peace and any sense of self-love run out of our spirits like liquid from a dying hose. But the lie that we believe isn't just that what we are isn't good enough; it's bigger and more destructive than that. The lie is that we *are* a "what."

Shhh. I hear it whistling.

Josh, you're not a person. You're a thing. You're a pathetic object, a simple and fading object. Do you see that one? That's better than you. Nicer. Shinier. Faster. Stronger. Smarter.

That makes you, well, you already know, don't you?

It's destructive, and if you think about it, it greatly explains why we can't seem to love ourselves. After all, the soul isn't wired to love things. Enjoy them? Yes. Like them? Yes. Find them meaningful? Sometimes. But love them? No.

One of the greatest reasons we don't love ourselves is because we don't see ourselves as people. We see ourselves as objects, so we don't find our value in *who* we are, but rather in *what* we are, *what* we can do, *what* we have, *what* we look like, and *what* we can offer. We've come to believe the lie, and because of it we're never good enough, because no object ever is. This is why new cars and computers are released every single year, because the old version has become substandard.

To be acceptable, it now needs more trimmings and better trappings. Enhanced brakes. Smarter GPS. More memory. Sharper cameras. Objects always need to be getting better. They need new paint. They need to be polished. They need to be faster. And if we see ourselves as objects, then we too must become a newer and better version of ourselves. Always.

It's not just because culture is progressing that plastic surgery, steroids, cosmetics, and tanning beds are such booming industries. It's because we feel so extraordinarily wretched about ourselves.

So in desperation, we turn to what we think, or what we're told, will change that and make us good enough, something of value—bigger boobs, darker tans, stronger muscles, leaner legs, younger skin, firmer abs, better clothing, and greater sex appeal. We don't necessarily want to; we have to. We have no choice. Otherwise, we're just a worse version of someone else, which is what Chris believed about himself.

In his mind, he was a "what," and the way he treated himself reflected that. He did whatever he thought he had to do in order to be good enough, to be better, to be worthy of love, and in his mind, the best way to do that was through a simple equation.

Chris
+ Hottest and most exotic-looking girl he can find
+ Have lots of wild sex and give her what she wants
+ Because she wants sex from Chris, he feels wanted
= Chris feels better and worth something and lovable

That was his formula, and he executed it to perfection. He found the exotic girl, they had lots of wild sex, and she wanted *what* he had. The only problem was what came after the equal sign. It didn't add up to Chris feeling better, to Chris feeling valued and loved. It added up to fear that she would eventually toss him aside like an outdated piece of technology. It added up to Chris hating himself even more. For him, even the perfect equation executed perfectly didn't take away the hurt of believing the lie.

Which brings me to truth, and Andy Dufresne.

Shawshank

One of the first films that both moved and disturbed me was *The Shawshank Redemption*. I watched it by myself and was a tangled mess of optimism and nausea afterward.

160

In the movie, Andy Dufresne is falsely imprisoned on charges of murder, but he decides that his stay behind bars will be a brief one. He's going to escape by digging through the thick rock prison walls. It's an ambitious idea, but the most improbable component to his plan is not the idea of escape, but the object that will allow him to escape.

He chooses a tiny instrument called a rock hammer, used primarily for carving stones into intricate figures. Each night, as the inmates and guards sleep, he chips away at the wall. Each scrape and each chip takes a small piece out of that rock wall. He repeats this ritual until finally, after years and years of tapping away, his tunnel reaches the outside, and he escapes. Through a myriad of tiny scratches, he is set free, and though it may not have been the ideal or the quickest way, it was the only way.

I've come to believe that truth is like that rock hammer. That by hearing it, being around it, and allowing it to move through our skin, underneath our muscles and tendons, and into our blood and heart, we can be set free, set free from the Artificial Paradise. After all, it's not simple behaviors that keep us trapped. It's more than that. It's our belief. It's our belief in a lie.

The lie traps us. The truth frees us.

But I've also come to believe that, like that rock hammer, truth often chips away at lies, rather than bashing through them with one gigantic swing, like a wrecking ball. It has to come across us time after time, and each time, a little more of that lie is scraped away.

For me to find freedom from self-hate, I had to come across it more times than I can count.

I can't get into all of it, because I promised myself that this book would be shorter than it already is; but if I did, I'd tell you all about how I hated myself. I'd tell you how I believed that I

161

wasn't, and would never be, good enough, not at anything. I believed I would always be too skinny, too ugly, too stupid, too plain, too uninteresting, too disappointing, too predictable, and too everything else that I didn't want to be. I'd tell you about how, for a long time, I treated myself accordingly.

That era of my life is a dim one that includes steroids, weekly cutting, heavy sadness, and lying about it all.

But then I'd tell you all about how God spoke to me, both directly (once while I was on a stormy mountain peak in Colorado and once while I was lying on the floor in my bare, furniture-less apartment), and through a group of people. They weren't always the same people; sometimes it was a friend or a pastor,[1] sometimes it was an author,[2] other times it was a musician[3] or a filmmaker. But I'd tell you how both they and their creations encouraged me persistently and consistently, when I needed it most. I'd tell you how they spoke unstoppable words of truth and inspiration, and words that called me out to change the way I lived.

I'd tell you how those concrete lies slowly became brittle, how they cracked, and how they finally broke. I'd tell you how God dug me out, how I now have a greater sense of freedom[4] from the Artificial Paradise thanks to God, truth, and the people who, like Andy Dufresne, were patient and courageous enough to offer freedom to me through a million little scrapes.

But I don't have time, so let me tell you how I've seen Chris set free in a similar way.

Happy to Hold Condoms

For months, when we hung out, I got to play a small part, like those who freed me, in scratching at the lies with truth. It was pretty simple, really. I encouraged him. I put into words the incredible things I saw in him, and the promises of Scripture, and believed that on some mystical level, God was digging him out. Each time we were together, I did it. After a while I became a broken record.

"You know what, Chris? I really like hanging out with you."

"Yeah, I know," Chris would say.

"Chris, I see God working in your life."

"Okay, Josh. Thanks."

"Chris, I really care about you."

"Chris, God is crazy about you."

"Chris, you're really smart."

"Chris, God wants you to use your gifts and talents."

"Chris, God did an incredible job creating you."

"Chris, I love hearing you laugh."

"Chris, I pray for you all the time."

"Chris, God loves you and you know why? Because you're Chris."

Like I said, a broken record: repetitive, even annoying, and definitely simple.

But I suppose that's not unlike God. He likes to repeat himself too. A lot.

"I love you."

"Here's how much I love you."

"Again, I love you."

"I'd do anything for you. Because I love you."

"Because I love you, I'd do anything for you."

"I'm here for you."

"I'm still here for you."

"Even now, I'm here for you."

Over and over and over again, God says the same things. I don't think it's because his memory is slipping with old age, or anything like that. I think it's because he is acutely aware of how persistent evil is, and of how often we need to hear encouragement in a world where we are so consistently blasted with messages that tell us otherwise.

So being repetitive isn't a bad thing. It's a wonderful thing, a necessary thing.

Over the next year, Chris and I spent a lot of time together, and I spent a lot of time scratching and scraping, a lot of time praying for God to dig Chris out. Then I actually got to see it begin to happen. A crack slowly formed, and soon after, I saw that crack become a break, and then, one Wednesday afternoon, I got to see that break give way to fresh air and daylight.

Chris sat in a chair across from me. He hunched on his knees, rubbing his hands. At one point he was rubbing them so hard they started to turn deep pink. His feet were tapping on the ground, fast, like a sewing machine. Bum Bum Bum Bum Bum Bum.

He's thinking about something. That's obvious. What's he about to say? I wonder if . . .

His head rose slowly, like a sunrise.

"Josh," he said, taking a deep breath, "I don't want to live like this anymore. This isn't who I want to be, and this isn't how I want to see myself."

He reached into his back pocket and pulled from it a pair of condoms, and taking my hands, gave them to me. Two Trojans. Ribbed. For her pleasure. I've never been happier to hold a pair of condoms in my entire life.

Chris still has jet-black hair and that infectious laugh, and now he's growing to love himself, as God loves him, and as he does, he's healing. He's beginning to believe the truth about himself, beginning to see himself the way God sees him.

Lovable. Created. Person.

That Gravelly Road/Hate/A Dark Alley/Divisions/Brother/God's Dream

Free-Flowing Thoughts on Undisrupting a Disrupted World

Kristen and I were in the airport. I love airports. Being in one always means that I'm going somewhere. Prior to boarding the plane we were perusing the bookstore looking for some in-flight reading material. I stooped past the book section, most of which was stocked with Rachel Ray cookbooks and Joel Osteen's face, and wandered into the magazines and newspapers. Glancing across the menagerie of titles, my eyes landed on one specific cover.

The headline, "It's over," was stamped on a blue and pink magazine and the photograph pitted two Generation Y celebrities against each other, with a thick black line down the middle, visually capturing the alleged division.

Opening the cover, I flipped through the pages, and read all about the collapse of the once strong relationship. Antagonistic quotes, sopping with bitterness and hurt, littered the exhaustive and detailed article up until the very last paragraph. I closed the magazine and, not about to pay five dollars for it, set it down. Then I continued looking around that airport bookstore, and after just a few brief minutes, I saw a striking pattern, shining on me like a constellation punctured in the dark sky.

Envy, discord, hate, anger, and bitterness headlined magazine after magazine and newspaper after newspaper. Divorces. Splits. Rifts. Break-ups. Break-offs. Distances. These headlines came from all areas of culture and life. Division was everywhere, forgiveness was nowhere, and a cold and overwhelming reality about my generation hit me like it never had before. Unity amongst us has been disturbed, greatly disturbed. Something has gone horribly wrong and we now find ourselves a generation of broken communities, broken families, and lost relationships.

Standing there, I began to think about the people in my life, friends of mine whose lives are marked by this disruption.

John—dabbles in Buddhism—completing his PhD—Divorced. Candace—super intelligent—dark hair—refuses to talk to her in-laws—Bitter. Kassie—sweet—hospitable—looks like a movie star—comes from a broken home—Hates her step-dad. Rich—military man—bodybuilder—wife served him papers while he was leading troops in Iraq—Divorced. David—rides dirt bikes—family man—Runs from church communities when they ask a lot of him. Sonja—wealthy family—absolutely hilarious—cheated on her husband multiple times—Divorced. Sean—worship leader—courageous—Won't talk to his best friend anymore because of a financial dispute. Tara—servant—would do anything for anyone—works in a church—Won't talk to her best friend anymore because of, well, because of no good reason. Ellen—kind of a hippie—creative spirit—refuses to talk to her mom anymore—Can't seem to forgive. Haley—honest—driven like few are—Runs from relationships at the first sign of trouble.

And those were just a few of the names and circumstances that came to mind in the airport bookstore.

We are a shattered generation, a people low on unity and high on division, low on forgiveness, and high on both resentment and hate. It's all around us. It's in us, and it's eating away at us, ripping us apart, and killing us softly. Staring into the extent of this reality, I sometimes feel like I've reached a dead end, a claustrophobic passageway, with no way out.

> *It's damp. Smells like mildew and decomposing leaves. The lights above me flicker on and off. Onoff. On off. On......................*
> *off............*
>
> *......................................On.*

> *A drop of something lands on my shoe. Where am I? I'm in a long dark alley. I look everywhere for a way out, but I see none. A drop of something lands on my shoulder.*

> *I run ahead, and frenetically pet the walls, hoping to find a hatch, a door, a window, a ladder. But I find none. A drop of something lands on my hair.*

> *I can't get out. These faded, red brick walls won't let me. Like bullies, they stand over me. They wear sharp barbwire like a top hat, and they taunt me. A drop of something lands in my eye.*

> *There's no way out, no way out of this disrupted existence.*

Sometimes I feel like it will always be this way, like my generation will forever sit underneath the twinkling of that ugly constellation. On some level, that's true.

Disruption, hate, and resentment will always exist, but that doesn't mean that an individual, a community, or a nation can't be rescued. They can, and I've seen it. There is a way out of this disrupted existence. It's not easy, but there is a way that we can take to bring healing.

The way of oneness. Forgiveness. Reconciliation. Unity.

It's the only way out of that dark alley, the only thing that can reverse the damage.

If only we, as Christians, embodied them, others might be set free, which reminds me, because . . .

Thought I. Eavesdropping on People in Blockbuster Video

A few days ago I was standing in line at Blockbuster Video. I had made my video selection and I was quite pleased with it. So now, I was just waiting to check out. Behind me stood a couple having a conversation and I couldn't resist the temptation to eavesdrop.

"At some point I want to rent that Bible movie," she said.

"The Bible?" he asked. "You mean the book that makes everyone hate everyone else?"

"What are you talking about? I mean that Bible movie. I think it's called *Jesus Camp*."

She was a little irritated.

"Yea," he said smugly. "That's about the Bible, and haven't you ever noticed that after people read the Bible they always end up hating everyone else?"

At that point I paid the four dollars and hurried home to watch the movie I had rented. *Jesus Camp*.

On my way back, a red light, one of those stubborn red lights that refuses to turn green, stopped me. I sat there for what felt like twenty minutes, and thought about the conversation I had just overheard. I couldn't help but consider how accurate the assertion seemed, the assertion that people that read the Bible end up hating everyone else, that Christians are so hate-filled.

While we don't tolerate sexual immorality, cursing, or substance abuse, we, as Christians, have made a habit of justifying rifts, withholding forgiveness, and harboring tiny seeds of hate, refusing to relinquish bitterness towards those who have wounded us, betrayed us, and given up on us. It's hard to see God in that. In fact, it's almost impossible to see God in that.

For a moment I thought the light was going to turn green. It flirted with it. I think it wanted to turn green. But it didn't. I took my foot off the brake anyway, and let the car roll forward a few feet, just so I could feel like I was moving. It came to rest again, and then I thought about how when Christians live as one, God can be seen so clearly.

God is the perfect embodiment of oneness. It's like that verse in the Old Testament says: "Hear O Israel, The LORD our God, the LORD is *one*!" (Deut. 6:4). While he is three distinct beings—Father, Son, and Spirit—together those beings form *one*. In oneness God is seen.

So when the church, many parts and many people, exist and function as *one* body, like God dreams, God is seen. When two unique people join together in marriage to form *one* flesh, like God dreams, God is seen. When those we disagree with, believe differently than, have bad histories with, and have been wounded by come together with us as *one*, like God dreams, we reflect God and in that, God is seen.

That's what my generation needs in order to heal. We need to be shown God.

169

We need to see what mad-forgiveness looks like from mad-forgivers. We need to see someone persevere through betrayal, people unapologetically and unswervingly devoted to unity, no matter how hard it might be. People need our willingness, your willingness, to pursue reconciliation one relationship at a time, one moment at a time, because seeing that awakens something, something stronger than hate and stronger than separation. It awakens the thumbprint of God and his dream for oneness embedded deep within all our hearts.

Finally, the stubborn light turned green, and I turned onto my street and pulled up the ramp into my building complex. As I did, I couldn't help but think of when . . .

Thought II. The Man with the Jagged Scar

I was passing through rural Texas. Rural communities are something that I know very little about, so I still have a certain naïve fascination with them. Even now, when I drive by a farm or ranch, I stare out the window at the crops, the silos, and the horses. I see black and white cows grazing and chewing grass, entirely carefree, completely at ease, and I'm strangely jealous of them, enamored with that life. It's like I can't believe this whole other world I'm so unfamiliar with is that close to me.

The reason for my passing through was to speak at a conference, and at this particular conference I met someone I will never forget. I met a man who truly is a dreamer, a man whose life has brought tremendous healing to my generation, myself included, because it offers this very picture of oneness, of God's dream. I don't remember his name. Come to think of it, I don't know if he ever gave it to me, so rather than referring to him as "that guy," let's just call him Sir.

Sir approached me on Saturday night, at the conclusion of the conference, and his face instantly held my usually meandering attention. The left side bore a jagged scar that spanned from above his eyebrow to just above his cheek, passing directly over his left eyeball, or where his eyeball should have been. It wasn't there. It was gone, replaced only by a mangled socket.

"You talked a lot up there about unity and forgiveness," he said in a gruff but soft voice as we shook hands.

"Yea, I guess I did. What'd you think?" I said.

"Well, I believe in those things. I believe in them a lot. I believe that they're important, and that they're important to God."

"That's great. Is there a particular reason why you believe that?" I asked.

Sir's right eye now fixated on me like a blowtorch, as if attempting to burn right through me.

"I have a story for you, Josh," he said.

Now before I continue, allow me to offer some relevant advice that I learned from the American cinema.

"There are three rules that I live by: never get less than twelve hours sleep; never play cards with a guy who has the same first name as a city; and never get involved with a woman with a tattoo of a dagger on her body. Now you stick to that, and everything else is cream cheese."

Brilliant words from Coach Flinstock in the movie *Teen Wolf*. I can't believe I'm quoting *Teen Wolf*. Actually, yes I can. I love that movie.[1] But I'll add one more to his list. If a guy with a jagged scar on his face tells you he has a story, you listen. So I did as Sir told me his fateful story of the soggy Florida everglades.

It went something like this. Two old-time buddies looking to relive their nostalgic college days go on a fishing trip, for a

171

week of laughs, conversation, memories, sport, and a general sense of escape from everyday adult life and responsibility. It began just as planned and continued as a picturesque adventure. It was everything that they hoped it would be for the first couple of days. But it was gruesomely and unexpectedly interrupted when Sir's friend brutally stabbed him in the chest with an ice pick and then shot him in the head. With the life draining out of his body, Sir's friend took everything—the boat, the supplies, the laughs, and the nostalgia—and left him for dead in the muggy wilderness.

Listening, I was hypnotized, completely under his control. With each word adding to the story, it became more and more difficult for me to swallow or collect my thoughts. In hindsight, there are a million questions that I wish I had posed to Sir at this point.

How did you get to the hospital? What kept you alive? Why on earth did your friend put an ice pick in your chest and shoot you? You didn't deserve it, did you?

Josh, you idiot, no one deserves that.

But I was so enthralled with every word that the questions didn't even cross my mind.

As the conference auditorium emptied, Sir continued, sharing the hate and anger that billowed in his heart towards his friend/attacker, both throughout his recovery and following. He shared about the bitterness. He shared about the sorrow. He shared about his intense appetite for revenge and retaliation, and he shared about his powerful rage. He shared about how over the years it slowly rotted his heart, about how it was destroying him, his relationships, and his relationship with God. But then Sir spoke of something more. He spoke of the work God did.

He told me about the softening of his heart, the lifting of hate, the healing that happened within him, even to the point where he privately forgave his friend. I was completely blown away and loved the fact that his horrific story had such a great ending. But as it turned out, that wasn't the ending. Sir wouldn't let that be the ending. He hungered for more. He burned and dreamed of unity too strongly for the story to end there.

Years later, as Sir's former friend lay in a hospital on his deathbed, just days from eternally sinking from this world, Sir ventured back into his worst nightmare, into his most painful memory. Sir paid his former friend a visit. And Sir looked directly into the face of the man who took his eye, the man who had left him for dead . . . and he forgave him. He told his attacker to his face, "I forgive you for what you did." They sat, together. They talked, together. Reconciliation of the most impossible kind happened and, before his friend died, Sir led the man that attempted to kill him into a relationship with Christ.

If that's not a picture of God and his dream, then I don't know what is. If that doesn't awaken something in us, then something is wrong. Sir absolutely shines God and shows me what God looks like in a disrupted world. His life breathes hope into my divisions, my bitterness, and offers me the often-hard-to-believe truth that the possibility of forgiveness, healing, and oneness is never dead, NEVER dead, NEVER dead, NEVER dead, and reminds me in such a convicting, inspiring, and stirring way that . . .

Thought III. Oneness Is a Gravelly Road

God wants reconciliation. Always. No matter the hurt or let down, no matter the depth of the betrayal or the weight of the grievance, regardless of if it's small or massive, He wants us to forgive, to let go of bitterness and anger so that we all can heal.

So maybe the question now is, whom do you need to forgive? Whom do you need to reconcile with or let go of bitterness with?

The successful or drop dead gorgeous or talented person. The person who spoke venomous words about you, words that cut you, hurt you, or even ripped your heart wide open. The person who won't let conflict die, just brings it up again and again, and hangs it over your head. The person who abused you or someone you love. The person who ignored you, abandoned you, discarded you, or forgot you. The person/people who believe differently, live differently, and think differently than you. Ex-boyfriend, ex-girlfriend, ex-husband, ex-wife, current husband, current wife, ex-parent, parent, ex-colleague, ex-friend, friend.

It might not happen in one fell swoop. It might not all happen today or tomorrow. In fact, a lot of times, it probably won't. That's okay, and I think it's okay with God.

For him, the road of oneness is a paved, well-lit, five-lane freeway that takes one step to travel. When I've hurt him, hated him, and divided myself from him, we become one again before what I desire in my heart can be put into words. With him, forgiveness and unity is quicker than instant . . . But I'm not him. I'm a broken person, and often it takes time for a broken person to do something this divine.

For me, the road of oneness with others doesn't seem to be paved. It seems to be a winding gravel road, overgrown with prickly weeds and poisonous plants. It's covered in a blanket of ominous black rainclouds that never cease to hover and drip. This road is jammed with confusing detours and is poorly lit, so poorly that I can hardly see ten feet in front of myself. It's a road I get lost on, a road that sometimes gets flooded and closed. It's a tough road, a painful, wrenching, and impossible feeling road, and traveling it is daunting. But thankfully, it's a road God is willing to walk with me, and all of us. He is willing to stumble and weep with us down that gravelly road. Our role is simply the willingness to go with him, no matter where we are.

So let him stand next to you as you look at the road from a distance. Ask him to walk with you that one step. No matter where you are, invite God to meet you and walk from there. Pray, plead, acknowledge, and confess that disruption in your heart, ask for the strength, and do it again tomorrow, because you'll probably have to. Let God shape you into a person who desires forgiveness, reconciliation, and unity. Let God shape you into a dreamer, and one who goes to great lengths to achieve it. As he nudges you down that gravelly road, respond with that next step.

Respond, and God will use you to heal others in my disrupted generation, just like he's used Sir to heal so much of the bitterness and division in me.

It all began when I was . . .

Thought IV. How Josh Lost His Tail

Growing up, I lived under the same roof with two sisters, Corbett[2] and Quinn.[3] They are special people—storytellers, adventurers, travelers, writers, actresses, and dancers. As kids, we attended the same schools and spent much of our free time together, doing all sorts of odd things: dancing like Michael Jackson, whining when our parents dragged us to flea markets, and enduring long family van rides to the Iowa Corn Palace and Mount Rushmore.

Along with Corbett and Quinn, I also have a half brother and a half sister from my Dad's first marriage whom I rarely ever spoke to or saw. I don't know exactly why that was the case, but I think it was, in part, simply the age difference

175

between us. Kraig and Kelly are both more than a decade older than me, so our life stages were pretty different, along with our interests. But that's not the only reason.

My mom was always reluctant to bring all of us together. There was some lingering resentment there for her, I think, coupled with a fear of how the Christian community might respond to it. She and my dad were both previously married, and they started dating before my dad was divorced, so I guess she just didn't want to deal with the questions, the scowls, and the whispers. Regardless of the reason, not spending time with Kraig and Kelly was always just fine with me. In fact, I didn't want anything to do with them, especially Kraig.

He looks like my dad, a Burt Reynolds throwback, tall and handsome, with eyes like moons and a stern jaw. He knows how to put up drywall, level floors, and dig trenches, and he can name more than ten tools that everyone should have in their garage. He played football for Purdue University, and after graduating became a successful building developer who helped construct some of the most celebrated structures in and around the Chicago area.

The Trump Tower. The United Center. The Joliet Speedway.

My dad was so proud of Kraig and spoke about him and his accomplishments often, about how the *Chicago Tribune* wrote a story about him and how he received a handwritten thank you letter from Donald Trump for his outstanding work on his new hotel. I imagine that's part of why I didn't want to spend time with him. Compared to him, I felt like the lesser son, and I resented him for it.

He was opening letters from billionaires and I was in counseling for depression. He was a Division I athlete who competed against future professionals, and I was the sixth man on my high school basketball team. Over time my resentment, envy, hate, or whatever else you want to call it, grew, and as it ate away at me, I pushed Kraig farther and farther away. So much so that when I got married, we hadn't spoken to each other in more years than I could remember and I didn't even invite him, or Kelly, to my wedding. But in spite of that growing chasm, my dad always attempted to build a bridge between us. He wanted so badly for us to have a relationship.

When he was having dinner with Kraig I was often invited to come along. I, of course, always had a convenient excuse for not going, but he remained persistent. Every year he tried to get us together for Christmas or Thanksgiving. That conversation was almost a signal that the holiday season had arrived.

"Josh," Dad would say hopefully, "I'm going over to your brother's house for Thanksgiving. I'd love for you to come with. Would you?"

"Nope," I would say, as I looked at the floor, shuffling out of the room and thinking.

It must be the holidays again.

My hate and bitterness stayed with me for a long time and killed me as it did, but one morning, everything began to change.

God's hand led me there. Nothing else really explains it. I woke up earlier than I had been, and felt like lying in bed. Feeling the cool sheets around my feet takes me back to my childhood and reminds me of my Star Wars pillowcase and comforter. But for some reason, I didn't stay in bed that morning. I went to the hospital instead. Stepping into the room, it was evident what was about to happen. It's weird, but death has an unmistakable feeling. It's almost like you can touch it, or maybe like it touches you. That feeling told me that my father, who had been fading from life that whole week, had only a few minutes left.

I sat down to his right and placed his hand in mine. It was tinted navy blue, and cold. His breaths were labored and deep, and his eyes rested closed, never moving. This was the end, a final goodbye, and on the chance that he could still hear me, I wanted to ease any lingering worry he might have.

"You did really good, Dad," I said. "It's okay to go now. We're all going to be okay."

It may sound strange, considering the circumstances, but I wanted that moment to last forever. It was just my parents and me, and the only time I remember holding both their hands at the same time. And I knew it would be the last time. Then the door opened with a silence-slashing creak.

Kraig.

Without saying a word, he sat at my dad's left side, soberly taking his hand. In silence, we waited. His breaths grew shorter, fainter, and farther apart as if he was winding down, like a clock. In just a few short minutes he slipped away and died.

I sat there and didn't move. I just held my dad's hand and cried with my mom, nearly forgetting that Kraig was even there. I looked across my dad's body at him, and I watched him for a moment.

He looks more like my dad than I remember from the grainy pictures. But he doesn't just look like him. His presence feels like him. I see a tear.

He's crying. He cries like him.

I stole a brief glance back at my dad's absent face and I knew that it was time. I knew that it was time to step onto that gravelly road.

Releasing his cold hand for the last time, I stood up, and moved to the other side of the bed. It only took ten steps to get there, but it felt more like one hundred miles. Kraig looked at me and I opened my arms, and dropping my dad's left hand, Kraig stood, and took hold of me. He grabbed me, pulled me in strong and full, like my dad used to when he was younger. We both cried. We wept as two little boys losing their childhood hero, their daddy.

But that's not the only reason I wept.

I also wept for the years that I wasted on my resentment, the years that this division had cost us. I wept for the conversations, the jokes, and the brotherly fights that my hate had cost us. I wept for the chance to sneak into late-night R-rated movies, the debates over best athletes, the shared tears over another Cubs collapse, and the mid-summer barbeques that had all been lost. And I wept for the fact that my dad never saw us act the way that, for all those holiday years, he had hoped we would.

For the remainder of the day, we stayed at the hospital, comforting one another, trying to make sense of our lives, and talking to doctors and counselors. Before we left, Kraig invited me to swing by his house during the week. I accepted. I wasn't sure if I wanted to, but I did, and that Wednesday, I pulled into Kraig's driveway.

I felt like I was on a first date, only the most intense first date I'd ever been on. I was sweaty. Unsure. Nervous. Every organ in my body was changing positions. Stomach in my throat. Heart in my thighs. Brain dribbling from my ears. Lungs lost somewhere in the middle.

I walked slowly to the door.

Okay, if things start to go badly, I've got to have an escape plan. Actually, I could leave now. Maybe I should. Some of this could be potentially awkward. Hard. Ugly even. Maybe this is too soon? I don't want this bitterness anymore, but I've grown accustomed to it. It's a part of me.

179

It's my tail.

It wags back and forth when I'm excited, and when I'm scared or nervous it falls between my legs. That's where it is now.

Okay, here we go.

He met me at the door with another hug and welcomed me into his home. His wonderful wife, Brit, smiled and hugged me too, and then I met their three boys, my three nephews. After some introductions and high fives, Kraig escorted me onto the back porch where we sat in comfortable lawn chairs and cracked open two frosty beers.

"So, how long you guys been in this house now, Kraig?"

"Oh, it's been a while now."

"I love it, and I love this setup you have out here. Tons of space. It's probably great for boys, right?"

"Yeah, it works really well."

It was quiet for a moment.

"Kraig," I said, kind of slowly and kind of hesitantly, "I was really nervous about coming over here tonight."

"You were?" Kraig asked. "I was nervous too, but I'm really glad you're here."

"Yeah. I'm glad too," I said. "I think it's right, you know?"

"Yeah, I do."

He nodded, took a swig, and smiled back at me, his little brother.

As the night hours passed, we talked about the chasm between us, whether or not we look alike, our mutual love of Chicago, how we met our wives, and of course, Dad. I won't lie to you, it was a difficult night, really hard, but it was also incredibly healing and freeing, and it remains a constant reminder for me of how God dreams it to be.

Since, Kraig and I have continued our relationship. We spend time together whenever I'm in the Chicago area, we exchange emails and phone calls when I'm not—oh, and we've spent some holidays together now too. And as we've continued that relationship, as we've pursued God's dream, I've continued healing. The harbored bitterness and envy that ate away at me for so long has vanished. After many years of dragging it behind me, it's gone and I can now say that I'm so proud of my big brother, for all he's done, for who he is, and who he's still becoming.

I'm so thankful for his willingness to forgive me for all the years that I pushed him away, and that willingness has shown me God, just as Sir's willingness did, and through his willingness to forgive me, more healing is spreading, and that makes me think about my friend . . .

Thought V. A Contagious Dream

Ellen, one of the individuals I mentioned earlier, recently sent me this note after I shared with her the story of my brother and me.

> Thank you, Josh. I really needed to hear what you said to me this weekend. It was both convicting and inspiring at the same time. As you know, I haven't seen my mom in over a year or even talked to her in almost nine months, which went horribly, by the way. Dealing with it and her is so hard for me, but I just wanted you to know that in the next season of life, I'll be loving my mom. In the same way that you're choosing and trying to love your brother, I'll be loving her.

That's God's dream in one more person, and as Ellen continues down that path with her mom, oneness is waiting, newness is waiting, and healing for her hardened heart is waiting. But can you imagine how this generation might be changed if person after person were to walk that gravelly road and live a picture of God's dream? Can you picture the healing?

I can. And it's magnificent.

I'm back in that alley again, the one with no way out. The lights continue to flicker.

On.............off..............On.

A drop of something lands on my lips and I see an object that I didn't see before, a pure white brick, resting, practically hovering, in the corner.

I lay my hands upon it, and it glows brighter, and pressing it, it sinks into the wall, opening a door to another place, but this new place isn't another dark, narrow alley. I walk through the door into a . . .

. . . vast field.

There is a freshness in the air, the aroma of healing.
I see couples seeking to stay together, not just not divorcing, but truly loving each other and giving themselves to each other. I see children forgiving parents and parents embracing children, instead of pushing them away. I see professionals relinquishing bitterness toward employers that screwed them over and I see denominations standing as one, differences and all. I see individuals committed to community, instead of running, friends

talking through issues and communicating, instead of becoming enemies, and I see brothers living as brothers.

I see hate dying, bitterness fading, divisions ending, forgiveness increasing, reconciliation multiplying, love reigning, and unity constant. I see oneness.

I see God's dream.

And with every person that embodies God's dream a little bit more, healing comes, change comes, and this disrupted generation becomes a little more undisrupted.

Now where was I again? Oh yeah. Kristen and I were in the airport . . .

Wetlands

Guarding the Soul for Everyone's Sake

Hey, it's me.

But chances are, that doesn't really help.

I'm quite sure you don't recognize my voice anymore, which is tragic, because you used to. There was a time when we were friends, the best. We leaned against wooden fences and shared ideas. We sat in the grass and dreamed of seeing the whole world, writing poetry and songs, and changing this place. We believed in each other and nothing came between us. Not even air or time. This world looked different because of us . . . but everything is different now.

I'm a stranger to you. You hardly even recognize me anymore. We no longer sit together, leaning against wooden fences, and I can't recall the last time we felt the grass underneath our feet and jotted rhymes. You have no idea what I'm thinking about or what makes me soar. I don't think you're intentionally ignoring me, or anything like that, but I know what this world does to you, and what that, in turn, does to me. You get caught in the sticky web of every day, the small and repetitive, the minutia, the "have to get dones," as you call them. And somehow, while it's remembered, I'm forgotten.

Don't worry, I'm not here to whine or complain, but I'd be lying if I said that I didn't miss you. I do. Deeply. I miss chasing things of beauty with you, seeing your face light up and seeing the world light up through you. I miss knowing that you are becoming everything you can become. Anyway, now I'm rambling.

I'm your soul.

And I thought you should know that I'm dying . . .

I remember listening to Erwin McManus. He's a pastor in California and an author of multiple books that have found their way into my hands at the right time. I love him. In addition to Christian Bale, he is my man-crush,[1] and I have no problem admitting that. During this particular message, he was talking about maximizing your impact, and one specific phrase has remained with me.

He said, "It's best for the world that you are healthy."

I thought that was very profound, something that I typically forget. In the bubble of Christianity, sometimes I view taking care of myself as selfish, but the reality is, if my soul, mind, and body are healthy, I'm not the only one who benefits. Everyone benefits. Caring for myself can actually be a very selfless act.

That's changed the way that I look at one of the more famous proverbs, Proverbs 4:23. "Above all else, guard your heart, for it is the wellspring of life."

My heart is the wellspring of life, but not just my wellspring, like I often think. It's everyone's wellspring. It's for everyone. My heart affects the hearts of others, so it's imperative that I guard it, not only so that I can live fully, but also so that others can live fully, so they can drink of the joy and peace bubbling within it. If I refuse to heed the wisdom of the Proverbs writer, that spring dries up, and when that happens, no one drinks.

No one.

I think this is a part of why so many people, so many in my generation, remain so thirsty and broken, because we, as individual people, friends, and leaders, aren't caring for ourselves. Our hearts are drying up, growing more and more desolate, and as they do, the hearts of others grow more and more desolate with us. And desolate hearts aren't the ones used to bring change.

People God uses for change are those with hearts that are guarded—wetland hearts, swampy hearts, hearts saturated with an undeniable sort of life, running-over hearts, hearts that spend so much time swimming they get wrinkled and pruney, hearts that are submerged beneath a waterfall after the chests containing them have been cracked wide open. Those are the hearts my generation needs, so I have to guard my heart.

Not just for my sake, but for the sake of an entire generation.

Joining the Human Race

Dave and I went to breakfast, which is a tough thing for me to do. I love breakfast, but I hate waking up early. I'm more of a "crack of 10:00 a.m." kind of guy, but on this occasion I went anyway. We enjoyed some laughs along with great food—steak and eggs washed down with five cups of coffee for me.

At one point Dave's face adopted a more somber look, and then he asked me one of the most convicting questions I've ever faced.

"Josh, can you remember when you last took time to be human?"

"I'm not sure I know what you mean, Dave."

"Well, when's the last time you went out with your friends?"

He hesitated, and then continued, "When's the last time you really laughed? When's the last time you went on vacation or went to the movies? Do you have any hobbies? When's the last time you invested in that? You know, when's the last time you did something human?"

I put up my hands, letting him know that I understood the nature of his question. Then, setting down my cup of coffee, I slowly brushed the carnage of torn sugar wrappers and crumpled blue cream containers across the table, without saying a word.

"That's what I thought," Dave said. "You haven't taken the time to be human in a while, have you?"

He knew just like I did. I hadn't. I couldn't remember the last time I had done any of the things Dave mentioned, at least not with any regularity.

At that time, I was out loving people constantly. Every day, from the time my head bumped off the pillow, I met with individual after individual and group after group, mostly over meals and cups of coffee. It's a miracle I didn't double in weight, have three heart attacks, or end up as a testimonial on a Richard Simmons infomercial. If my day ever had down moments, they were spent preparing for speaking engagements, so even in the "down times," my mind kept working.

I'd typically return home sometime after 10:00 p.m., drag myself up the stairs, and collapse onto my tan couch that I called my bed. Then I'd get up the next morning and do it again. And there were few exceptions.

On consecutive years, I sat in my office at the church into the late evening on Christmas Eve, talking with people, staring at my computer screen, and valiantly attempting (but failing miserably) to come up with fresh, creative ideas. My Jeep would pull out of the church parking lot and arrive at my parents' house, snapping over the snow-covered driveway just minutes before Christmas Day. I always walked in just barely in time to savor the last few drops of eggnog and final moments of conversation before everyone fell asleep.

That was my life. That's what I had become.

I didn't know how to have fun. I didn't know how to relax. I didn't know how to do so many of the things that I really enjoyed. It seems like such a dumb thing to be bad at, but I was horrible at it, and there were consequences.

My friendships became shells of what they had been. I didn't have time for them anymore, or for most of my hobbies and leisurely joys. I didn't have time for anything. I was too busy.

Giving. Serving. Working. Leading.

Draining. Drying. Tiring. Wearing down. Breaking down.

The funny part about it is that I felt that my lifestyle carried a certain nobility. I knew I was tired and worn out, but so did others, and I liked the idea of people knowing that. They looked at me with such respect because I was willing to sacrifice myself for everyone else. I loved that look. After a while, I don't even think I continued at my pace in order to bring healing to others. I think I did it to get that look one more time. So I kept working, and in doing so, continued leaving the human race.

> All work and no play makes Josh a dry Martian.
> All work and no play makes Josh a dry Martian.
> All work and no play makes Josh a dry Martian.
> All work and no play makes Josh a dry Martian.
> All work and no play makes Josh a dry Martian.
> All work and no play makes Josh a dry Martian.
> All work and no play makes Josh a dry Martian.
> All work and no play makes Josh a dry Martian.

All work and no play makes Josh a dry Martian.
All work and no play makes Josh a dry Martian.

Others may leave the human race for alternate reasons—searching for validity, loathing stillness, or simply because we're workaholics—but whatever the reason, many of us do it. Nowadays it's so easy to fall into it.

Our world doesn't like slowing down. We are a world of productivity, of "getting it done," being the best, and over-achieving. If we aren't working, grinding, and pressing, someone else is, and that means we're falling behind, and that doesn't sit well with us or our employers. So we press and press and press ourselves, running like rodents in wheels, pummeling our heart, mind, and body to get "it" done (whatever it is) until we are no longer human. And though we may hear or like to think otherwise, it's not noble. It's irresponsible.

There's nothing noble about gouging your soul by working too much. There's nothing noble about neglecting your family or erasing fun and joy from your life. There's nothing noble about churning until you have nothing left to give, and then churning more. There's nothing noble about not having hobbies and ignoring the Sabbath.

There's nothing noble about leaving the human race, and yet, many of us have. Have you?

When's the last time you rested or really laughed?

What's your hobby or interest? Are you giving time to it?

When's the last time you exercised? watched an entire football game? wrote a song?

When's the last time you cooked your spouse breakfast in bed or put work off until later?

Two of the most dynamic people I know are also two of the most human people I know.

When I first came on staff at a church in Austin, I was a little worried about the work rate. It seemed really fast, too fast. New agendas were rolled out every month, and a pressure to keep up with the growing and needy community was high. I had been there for only a few months and was already spinning at my psychotic pace, when on a Friday afternoon, while hunkered down in my office and buried under a landslide of problems and people, an email from Ted, our teaching pastor, popped into my box.

"Hey. The boss is out for the day. Let's go eat wings and watch the Cubs game."

I sat there for a moment, wondering if it was some kind of "test" that the church suits were conducting to see which staff members would act naughty while our lead pastor was away for the day, so I didn't respond. I guess I wanted to be nice. But in my mind I thought, *Even if this email is legit, I can't take off. The world needs me to do my work. I need me to do my work. I have to keep up and remain ahead of everybody, or at least close. I work. This is what I do. This is what I do. This is what I am.*

A few minutes later, Ted, along with JJ, another staff member, showed up in my office, already licking their lips. They were on their way out to eat wings and watch the game, and now that I think about it, they didn't really ask me to go.

Instead, like Secret Service agents, they told me that I was working too much. They told me that I was going, and that I didn't have a choice. So I went. And for an afternoon, I got to be human with JJ and Ted. We ate hot wings, laughed, and watched the Cubs game while we "should" have been or "could" have been working.

Certain people don't agree with this. They work themselves into a tizzy over the idea of doing it, claiming that the kingdom is near and life is too urgent to waste time at Pluckers Wing Bar, but you know what? There was something incredibly kingdom-oriented about that afternoon.

The rest. The laughing. The friends. The Cubs.

My soul was refreshed, and in that, I took part in something very "kingdom." My heart was guarded that afternoon, thanks to Ted and JJ. I cared for one of this generation's water sources, instead of letting it remain dry.

What could be more kingdom than that?

Diarrhea of the Mouth

I have a friend who talks too much. From the moment we get together, he starts talking, and he doesn't stop until we part ways. It's impressive, really.

FAMILYFRIENDSHOLLYWOODGOSSIPHECANT-STANDTHISPERSONORTHATPERSONSOMETHING ABOUTTHEUNITEDSTATESANDTHECAPITALOFDEL-AWARECHOCOLATETASTESGOODBUTHEHATES CHOCOLATECAKE. He just keeps going. Sometimes I have to do everything in my being to restrain myself from pounding the table and shouting everything that I'm thinking.

I wonder how hot this coffee is? Hopefully hotter than a thousand suns. Maybe I'll throw it all over you, just so you'll pause and take a breath. You'd have to then. Because you'd be melting. Maybe then I could get a word in.

. . . You still haven't stopped talking.

I love the guy, but it drives me crazy. People who interact this way drive all of us crazy, and we all seem to have one friend that does it. If you don't, then you might be the friend. The funny part is that when it comes to God, I was this friend.

When I was a teenager, I was taught to pray using the "ACTS model" of prayer (Adoration, Confession, Thanksgiving, Supplication). It was okay for a while, I guess, but of course, that prayer model, like so many, puts a zipper over

God's mouth. It's all about what I have to say and God listening to me. But that's how I prayed, every day.

God, forgive me for looking at that girl for longer than I should have, and forgive me for my jealousy. God, thank you for all you've given me—for my house and my family. God, you are holy and you are faithful. You're always there for me, and I love that about you. God, please watch over my friends. We all need you, and, oh yeah, work in my heart too. I've got issues. Oh, and do great things in this city. Amen.

That sounds like a decent prayer, and I suppose it is. I've got praise, thanksgiving, requests, and even some confession. Very well rounded. But, just like when I'm with my friend, in that kind of "conversation," only one of us has the chance to talk. And that's how God and I conversed. Over the course of fifteen or thirty minutes, I'd throw everything at God. Then I'd say Amen and be on my way, without giving him the chance to say one word.

My time in Scripture wasn't much different either.

I came at it to get what I wanted—the next insight, tidbit, or gem, and I'd move through it without stopping until I unearthed it. It was the snow and I was a snowplow, bulling over and through the words. Sometimes I would set a goal of reading through the New Testament in six months, or some other amount of time, and I'd plow away, never pausing or slowing down to listen. Oh, I learned a lot and was even filled by it. I could talk about more of it, but I never invited God to speak to me or guide me through it. I never saw or treated Scripture as God's mouthpiece to me. And it never even crossed my mind that my heart may be suffering as a result, dying even.

But my soul was dying, because by talking too much, living too loud, and failing to listen, I missed an essential of the heart. God's voice. Often, it is the most rejuvenating and encouraging thing in my life.

I frequently find myself longing for it, and simply hearing it gives me joy. It offers me comfort and it encourages me. It energizes, convicts, and directs me. God's voice is a cascade, the loosed fire hydrant on a sweltering August blacktop street, on my sweltering and parched spirit. Our hearts thirst for and need the voice of God, and God wants to speak to us.

He's personal like that. We're special to him like that.

God wants to talk to you, and he wants to talk to me. Of course, if I'm not listening, all of that becomes moot. It doesn't really matter.

Maybe that's why Jesus tells us to go into our rooms and close the door to pray. Maybe it's because unless we listen to someone, we're not really in much of a relationship. Maybe it's because someone can shout at me all they want while I'm in a crowded bar or at a casino in Vegas, but I probably won't hear them. I can't have great conversations there. Maybe Jesus is shifting how we approach God, moving us to an essential part of our relationship with him and our overall health. Listening.

I've learned a lot about listening to God through my friend John Burke.[2]

We were talking about the pace of his life and his relationship with God. He said, "You know, a few years ago I realized how much I talk to God about my life, the world, and what I want. I do it all the time, and then I realized how little I listen to God and what he wants to say to me. I rarely do that. Since that day I've begun listening to God, and I've never been the same."

As John shifted away from an ever-talking life to a more listening-oriented life, he experienced the tremendous fruit of it. He experienced how refreshing God's voice can be and he still does now. Today, John still frequently retreats to the

Pacific Ocean beach or into the hills on his mountain bike, just to listen. If you spend any time with him, you notice pretty quickly the courage, peace, and joy that pour out of him. You notice the Spirit kind of confidence. And while he benefits from that, so do I. And so does everyone else.

That's the kind of thing I need in my life. I need to become a listener, someone who retreats into my room, closes the door, and drinks of God's voice. While my travels aren't there yet, they continue to move in this direction. After years of suffering from raging diarrhea of the mouth and turning a deaf ear to God's voice, I'm finally listening.

Every morning while walking my dog, Ditka,[3] through a sleepy neighborhood, I pray. And other than the faint sound of speeding cars a few blocks away and the pitter-patter of lawn sprinklers, I'm hit with a muffled thud of silence. No phone. No iPod. No people. Just quiet. If there is something I have to get out to God, I get it out, but for the most part I say, *God, lend me your voice. I want to know about you. I want to hear from you. What's on your heart today, what's important to you? What are you thinking about? Speak to me.*

And then I just listen.

It's not like I've become a mime or anything. It's not that I don't ever tell God about what I want, vent to him, or confess and tell him that I love him. I do, but I guess the sound of my voice has become so sour compared to the sound of his, and this is true of my interaction with Scripture as well.

It's no longer always about finding what I want or learning something new. It's about hearing from God. I don't just want words. I don't want another nugget to carry around. I want the sound of his voice. I want him. So I'll sit at my desk, open my Bible,[4] and read.

Slowly. Quietly. By myself.

As I continue to move further into this life of listening, it seems that the exchanges with God that refresh my spirit most are those when I hardly utter a word. Simply hearing God's voice does so much more for the heart than hearing my own ever could.

Cave Dwellers

My friend Jon Peacock is one of the best friends I could ever ask for, and we know each other really well. The strange part is that we've spent less than a week together our entire lives. I've never experienced anything quite like it before, but somehow, we just know each other.

He is the architect of a Generation Y church community and is the perfect person for the job. In an area where people are utterly starved of community, he has a tremendous vision for it. And I mean a tremendous vision. His dream is that much of what we read about in Acts chapter 2 would be marrow to the lifestyle of that people.

He's not interested in planning neat events where people gather once a month for a pasta dinner and label it "life together." He wants people to share meals every single day. He isn't guiding people to have once-a-week small groups. He's leading them to move into the same apartment complexes, the same homes, and to engage in daily conversation and prayer with one another. And his vision is that followers of Jesus would do that with all kinds of people, from all kinds of financial backgrounds, ethnicities, and beliefs.

Now forgive me for stating the obvious here, but the kind of life that Jon is pushing people toward is abnormal. It's highly abnormal in our individualistic, self-sufficient, and isolated society. But Jon and his wife, Kelly, aren't doing it to be radical. They're doing it because they believe in it. They believe in the power of community and they're committed to living this kind of life.

I recently accepted an invitation to come to Chicago and spend two days with them, living in their home. We ate meals together, cried and laughed together, shared stories, prayed together, and talked about tasty wines. It was more than I could have ever asked for, and I'll remember it forever. I absolutely love being around them because Jon and Kelly have vibrancy in their spirits, a sparkling air of joy about them. And as the weekend went on, I found out why.

Sitting out on the back porch late one night, I bobbed in a rickety wooden rocking chair while Jon and I talked.

"I really like your place here, Jon. Very cool."

"Thanks a lot, man. Yeah, we like it."

He grinned and looked at the doors behind him.

"You think you guys will be here awhile?" I asked.

"Not really," he said, very sure of his answer.

"Oh, well, how much longer do you think you and Kelly will be here?"

"Actually, we've already decided. We're moving out in a few months."

"I had no idea. Awesome, man!" I said, rocking back and forth. "You guys moving into a bigger place?"

"Not really," Jon replied with a wave of gladness. "Actually, we're moving in with an older couple. They're in their sixties. We're really excited about it. They're amazing and we know that we're going to be challenged just by spending that much time around them. And I know we'll have a blast while we're doing it too."

As the last of Jon's words touched the night, I stopped rocking and realized something about him and Kelly.

Community-based life is not merely central to how they've chosen to care for my generation. It's central to how they've chosen to care for their own souls. Jon and Kelly have made the choice to tend to their own hearts, to be responsible enough to be held accountable, supported, and encouraged by others. This is in large part why their hearts are such refreshing springs, and perhaps why so many of ours aren't, and why mine often isn't.

People say that we become like our parents, and for some of us, that's a complete nightmare. Well, in this specific area of life, I'm living the nightmare. When it comes to community, I'm just like my dad.

Upon arriving home at night, he'd walk straight up the stairs into his bedroom and watch TV by himself, usually an old war movie or the Home Shopping Network. He did that every single night, for hours. From the time I was ten years old, I don't recall one instance when he spent time with a friend, not one. So, for my dad, there were no game days. No card nights. No men's breakfasts. No rec leagues. No double dates. He didn't have any community. And over the years, I've seen his pattern becoming mine.

My friends tell me all the time that I'm not "a hang out guy," and I suppose they're right. Unless we're doing something specific, I struggle to hang out. I don't just hang out. Actually, I hardly ever even answer my phone. But saying that I'm not a hang out guy can be putting it mildly. It's much more than that.

I am a cave dweller, showing myself only when I have to. I am Gollum.

People. People. People. People.

We smell them. They smell, smell like garbage! GARBAGE!!!

(Deep Breathing)

What do the people want? Yes, what??

(Deep Breathing) (Deep Breathing)

They want . . . us, our time. They want to giggle, hee hee, and play.

Nooo! NOOOOOO!!!!!!

We won't let them take it! Won't let them have us! We're ours! Not theirs . . .

(Deep Breathing) (Deep Breathing) (Deep Breathing) Ours.

(Deep Breathing) (Deep Breathing) (Deep Breathing) (Deep Breathing)

Have to sneak . . . have to crawl away . . . have to hide . . . have to protect it.

It's mine. My own. My precious.

For days at a time, I can be alone, which to an extent is good and part of who I am. It gives me space to think, create, and rest. But once I retreat too far into my reclusive world, I am smacked with repercussions, and so is everyone else. I get grumpy, distant, and insecure. I question whether or not people care about me. My creative flow is squelched, and I become susceptible to fears and temptations that otherwise wouldn't exist. A weird kind of paranoia sets in. If I stay in my cave too long, my heart inevitably, like the falling of leaves of autumn, begins to dry up.

My soul, as introverted as it might be, needs other people to stay hydrated. For my heart to breathe, I have to make the conscious choice to live communally, and I'm trying.

These days, I'm becoming more of a hang out guy. I'm spending time with my friends every week. We don't really have an agenda when we hang out. We just spend time to-gether, like normal people. We talk, eat, and watch movies. We help each other buy birthday presents for our wives and girlfriends, and we run errands. We ask each other hard questions, challenge ideas, and keep each other account-able. We pray together and for each other. We encourage each other, talk about how God is growing us, and what is frustrating us.

And you know what?

My life is fuller because of it. I need that kind of community. I need those friendships, and my generation needs me to have them, because the more I experience them, the more my heart evolves from a wasteland into a wetland. And then, everyone can drink.

The First Kid Picked

Coming to Terms with the Fact That Though God Does Some Really Crazy Stuff, He's Not Really Crazy

Recess is magical. Temporarily freeing children from posture-correcting plastic chairs, multiplication tables, and sterile rooms void of natural light, it is the jewel of the school day, a doorway into a fairy tale. Every moment holds the potential for untamed adventure, discovery, and spontaneous romance, all except for the moments of team selection.

It is the villainous stain on the midday frolic, the black cloud hovering over the princess's castle. It is an ugly process, by far the most miserable part of an otherwise enchanted hour.

Two of the coolest and most athletic alpha males stand as captains, in front of everyone, pacing back and forth, scanning the subordinate lineup of wannabes. The first to be picked are the best athletes, followed by the guys that kiss the butts of the best athletes, the Yes Men. You know these guys. They are the ones who claim to love whatever the alpha males love, and laugh at all their jokes.

I'm proud to say I was never in that group, at least not for very long. For the most part, I was just below it.

I fell somewhere between the shy, smart kid in the cotton Dockers who could catch the ball roughly half the time, and the kid who inevitably got his glasses knocked off on the first play, resulting in a bloody nose and a walk off the pitch while pushing back the tears. So while I wasn't a hot commodity, I was, at least, one of the guys that someone wanted, rather than the person that someone *had* to take just to even out the teams. But that person, the one who is taken just to even out the teams, is probably who a lot of us think we would be if God were the captain, picking his team to change this generation.

A lot of times, that's how I feel.

Sometimes I feel as though I'd be the last person standing there after all others have been taken, shamefully smearing the dirt underneath my Chuck Taylors as God and Jesus argue over who has to take me.

"Jesus, you take Josh," God says.

"I don't want him," Jesus says in a stern whisper that isn't quiet enough to keep me from hearing it. "Have you seen him play? He can't catch anything! You take him, God!"

"Oh yeah, like that's fair, Son! I'd rather play one short than have him."

I stand there, embarrassed. I feel unwanted. I hold my arms across my chest. I feel small, and that's good. This is one of the few times I wish I could go unnoticed. That would be better than this. But all is not lost, not yet.

I still hold the tiniest crumb of hope that one of them might want me.

Please take me. I know I'm not as fast or strong as the others. I'm not big or all that smart. But I'll try my best! Really! I hope that's good enough . . . oh, who am I kidding? They don't want me.

The crumb of hope falls from my hands.

A lot of times I feel like I'd be Mr. Even-Out-the-Teams. It's not so much because I don't think God can use me to do it. It's because of all the times that I haven't done it. It's because of all the times that I've chosen not to do it. It's because of all the times that I've even gone so far as to do the opposite.

Exhibit A:

Josh,

Ever since we talked recently, I've had some things weighing heavily on my mind, and I think that, in order to be fair to both of us, I should fill you in on them.

Since we were around each other consistently a few years ago, I've held onto a major grudge and even more hurt brought about by some of the ways that you interacted with me. Or didn't interact with me. It's been a few years, but even now when I think about it, I don't have peace. It still hurts and I'm not happy.

Basically, I felt as though I was on the backburner for you . . . like you never made much of an effort to have a relationship with me personally, but you were willing to make that effort with so many other people. And I guess in some ways I felt that the way the community you led interacted with me was a reflection of your interactions with me. I never felt embraced . . . by it or you.

I'm writing because I honestly believe that God is nudging me to say this to you. Obviously, it's been a long time since I've voiced these feelings, but the place they occupy in my heart remains a raw one, one that I don't like thinking about or talking about. My hope is not to make you feel bad or lecture, I just really need to get my feelings out to you so that you know what happened, that I'm hurting, and why I'm hurting . . .

Thank you for taking the time to read this, and again, I'm sorry that I never talked to you about this earlier. I guess I just never felt like it was the right time. I hope you are well, and that everything in life is working out for you.

Hopefully, I'll talk to you soon.

Abby

I've received some form of this email multiple times, and each time it's signed by someone that I've hurt in one way or another. Not exactly the guy you want when building a team to restore lives.

A Crown for the King

Taylor had a bowl haircut, a bad one. Not that there are good bowl haircuts. But his was especially bad. Still, it probably wasn't as bad as mine.

We knew each other in high school. He liked to draw and was great in front of people, always comfortable and confident but never condescending or arrogant. He had a way with words. They were always encouraging, to me and to everyone, and if you've forgotten the way that high school boys are, that's rare. I guess you could say that people caught a glimpse of the nurturing side of God through him, and that's wonderful.

But I couldn't stand it.

My neck temperature rose ten degrees when he was around, and when someone mentioned his name, it felt like a punch to the stomach. Taylor wore on me. He annoyed me and made me sick.

So did Matt.

Matt didn't have a bowl cut. His hair hung well below his shoulders and he often wore it in a ponytail. Not the awkward kind of ponytail fashioned at NASCAR events, but the artist kind. The Johnny Depp kind. It fit him well. Matt is a talented painter, photographer, and all-around amazing guy. Before we ever said hello, multiple friends of mine mentioned him to me, and everything they said was complimentary.

While they mentioned his talent and creativity, the thing I heard most was that he was a restorative force in the lives of people. I heard about how God was using him to touch lives all across Austin. I heard that he was loving, brave, honest, and compassionate. The stories about him came down like ticker tape at a parade, and with each one, that familiar feeling of disgust that I had around Taylor years before resurfaced. And it only heightened when we actually met.

As I got to know Matt and found him to be everything that everyone had said, that feeling was there, like a coarse black hair jabbing me in the eye, and just like it had with Taylor, that feeling kept me from celebrating Matt and wanting anything to do with him.

It might be confusing why I wouldn't want to be around people as great as these two, but it's actually quite basic. It's grotesque, but it is basic. Matt and Taylor took the attention off me.

Man, that's appalling to put down on paper and read with my own eyes. But it's so true.

The sick truth is that, at the time, I wasn't really interested in serving or seeing God bring change. I claimed that I was, and perhaps on the fringe of my spirit I was, but not at my core. At my core, I was my own greatest interest, and my passion was making my kingdom and myself greater. I wanted power. I wanted to be the center of everyone's universe. I wanted a crown and a gold-plated throne to sit on.

Like a king, I wanted to be admired, worshiped, and applauded, and people who did anything praiseworthy only got in the way of that. They took eyes and hearts off of me, and that made them my competitors, my enemies even. Matt and Taylor robbed me of what I wanted.

I see it so clearly now. I was a source of discord, a poison to both God's people and God's desires, and if I were him, that's not a person I'd take with any of my picks.

Ants Marching

Kristen and I live in the heart of Austin, just blocks from the University of Texas campus—home to somewhere over one hundred thousand young adults.

Our condo complex, a bohemian heaven, is located on a street referred to as "the drag" and is a total Generation Y mishmash. Except for the tenant above us, a mid-forties gentleman who for some reason has to drill early each morning, and the shy old man in 214, who drinks beer out in the courtyard every night and pleasantly nods to me whenever I walk by and say hello. It's a great place to live, and that's only cemented by the fact that it's built above a Chicago-style pizza joint and within walking distance of just about anything one could possibly want.

UT football stadium. Live music. Bike trails. Movie theater. Starbucks. Hippie grocery store.

I have a lot of memories from there, but one in particular stands out as being, well . . . I'll just tell you.

Sunday morning arrived, and after throwing on something close to clean, I walked out into the condo hallway to a peculiar sight: men in gray suits and uniformed police officers marching through the hallway like ants around their tunnels. Scampering up and down, they stepped in and out of my neighbor's condo, periodically stopping to whisper to each other. Navigating the obstacle course, I moved out of the building and into the warm sun, where I saw an ambulance, which, considering the presence of the police officers, was fairly predictable. But then I saw another vehicle, one I didn't foresee—a vehicle of a most unpleasant kind, four-wheel drive and dark navy blue. The shuddering words "Office of the Coroner" stamped on the side doors. That's when the nausea engulfed me.

As I glanced back over my shoulder down the T-shaped hallway, the bumblebee-colored police tape began to go up over my neighbor's doorway. A Generation Y law student in the fray of finals had committed suicide. The stress mounted until it swallowed him up, and he dealt with it the best way he knew how, by removing himself from it completely.

It's tragic. No, it's more than that. There are no words for it. What further adds to this tragedy is that as a follower of Jesus Christ, I never knew him, and each day we were only one door apart.

Each night, while my pillow caressed my head in its lap, we were separated by no more than five feet of concrete and drywall. We were so close to each other, but I never introduced myself, asked if he needed anything, or invited him to come over. During the day, I never paused long enough to walk thirty feet down the hall and knock, so I couldn't even tell you his name or what he looked like. I guess I was too busy.

Or maybe I just didn't care.

Love should have been right next door, but it wasn't; not from me.

I'm not fit for God's team. And yet . . .

Jesus is about to die. Guards have taken him by force and he's on his way to trial, humiliation, torture, and death.

If there's one time when you expect your friends to come through, that's the time. If there is one moment when you think that they will be there for you, it's then. Maybe they'll drop the ball when you have everything under control or they'll blow you off when things are status quo, but certainly not now. Now is the time when they have to be there, because you need them now more than ever! But as you probably know, Jesus's friends don't come through for him.

Instead, they desert him. All except Peter. Peter does more than just desert him.

As Jesus is taken in to see the high priest, a young girl approaches Peter.

"Wait a minute. I know you."

"You do?" Peter asks.

"Yeah, I do," she says with confidence. "You're one of the guys that was always with Jesus. Yeah, that's it! I knew I'd seen you somewhere! You're one of his disciples!"

"N-no. I'm not," says Peter, battling the suspicions of a gathering crowd. "I'm serious! I don't even know him!"

I'm not his disciple. I'm not his follower. I don't walk with him. I don't want to be like him. I don't represent what he represents. I don't love him.

Then, of course, as Jesus moves further into the worst moments of his life, that denial scene plays out two more times. And that's it. That's it for Jesus. He dies.

But I think something died in Peter too.

I think in that moment, hope died in Peter, and the belief that God could use him again. I think confidence and the dream that he would be the rock on which the church is built must have died. Chances are, he was preparing himself to hear Jesus, if he did come back, say, "Well, Peter, you had your chance and it didn't work out. So I'm going to go a different direction. But you know what? We do need even teams, so I kind of *have* to take you. So even though I don't want to, I will."

This was his biggest moment, and he blew it. At the most crucial time for him to come through, he didn't. Of all the characters and events of Scripture, it's easiest to see myself in this one. This one is so easy for me to relate to. I think I know how Peter felt here.

As you've read, I've had my own Peter moments. Moments when I could have come through, and I didn't. Moments when I needed to come through, and I didn't. Unloving moments. Arrogant moments. Cowardly moments. Hateful moments. And when those moments went down, there was that instant where something inside me died.

You probably know what I mean. I'm guessing you've had Peter moments too.

You've had moments where, like the Wizard of Oz, you've kept people who need to be let in, out, and moments when you've refused to let God change you. You've been a Champion. You've treated people like strangers, instead of like family. You've been a member of the Graceless Stampede, and pursued comfort over faith. You've been that arrogant street evangelist. You've bought into the Artificial Paradise. You've justified divides and hate in your life rather than dreaming like God, and you've neglected to guard your heart.

So you know the feeling Peter had in his gut, just like I do. And he had to sit with it for three agonizing days, waiting and wondering if Jesus was really going to return.

Of course, Jesus does return. He comes back to life and he's now ready to launch the church. He's ready to pick his team, and of all the disciples, and of all the people that he met over the course of his life, he can take anyone he chooses. Just like at recess, he can scan the yard and take whomever he wants.

Nicodemus. The Roman Centurion. John. Mary Magdalene. Another disciple. He can take anyone!

Then comes the twist.

O Captain, My Captain

Sitting on the beach, cooking fish over a crackling amber campfire, Jesus looks at his followers as they eat. Thinking. Imagining. And following breakfast, Jesus says, "Peter, do you love me?"

With passion, trying in vain to hold back the tears, Peter responds, "Yes. I do! I do! I—"

"Feed my sheep, Peter."

That's the twist. That's the moment when Peter's heart comes back to life.

Jesus picks Peter. First.

With his first pick to lead the church, Jesus takes the annoying kid who doesn't shut up. He takes the kid with the glasses and the frequent bloody noses. He takes the kid who's dropped nearly every potential game-winning pass. Jesus picks the kid who, just a few days ago, at the most crucial moment, blew it. He picks Peter. He picks Peter to lead his revolution of a broken world. And now, in the same way, God, the captain, picks us to continue his restoration of this broken generation.

He picks you, and he picks me.

It's recess again, and I've been on the monkey bars for a while, the blue ones. They are the short ones, close to the ground. Safer. I climb and I swing, but someone begins shouting. Loud. In a massive herd, everyone runs to the pitch. Oh no. Not again.

It's time to pick teams. Maybe this time it will be different. Maybe this time I won't get picked last. Yeah, right. God starts talking.

"Alright, I guess I'll go first."

He looks at everyone. Slowly. He doesn't look mad or intense. It doesn't really look like he's thinking about anything at all. It's almost like . . . like he just enjoys looking at us. At me even. He speaks again.

"I want Josh. I'll take him."

I'm not excited. There must be at least ten Joshes out here. That's a popular name. It's probably one of the other Joshes. I'm sure of it. He speaks again, and this time he's looking right at me.

"Yeah, Josh, I want you out here with me."

He smiles, like he believes in me, and he does. I don't know why. I don't care. I just run to him. I want to play alongside my captain. With my captain alongside me.

We play.

God picks me. He picks you.

It doesn't matter how many times we've blown it. It doesn't matter how slow and puny we are, how many passes have skipped off our stone hands, or how many times we've left the field sniffling because our glasses got knocked off. It doesn't matter how far off we feel we are from what people need, or how many people have been wounded by us through the course of our leadership. Right now, God, the captain, still picks us. He still picks me and he still picks you, but not because he has to even out the teams.

He picks you because he wants to. He wants you.

And that may be the strangest part of this. God uses the broken to heal brokenness. He picks those in need of change to bring change. He picks first the kids whom everyone else takes because they have to, to even out the teams, and somehow, God does the most incredible thing through them. He changes lives, making the broken into the beautiful.

He did it through Peter, and I believe that if we too, like Peter, are willing to walk with God deep into his heart, into our hearts, and into the hearts and lives of a generation, God will do equally stunning things in us and through us. I believe that through us—a group that under normal circumstances would only be used to even out the teams—God will write stories of healing and hope, stories that will take our breath away.

So serve. Lead. Live. Love.

Cry. Share. Rest. Hug.

Trust. Dare. Join. Invite.

Evolve. Stay. Go. Might.

Listen. Think. Believe. Shine.

Grace. Smile. Be. Dine.

Saturate. Strip. Break. Bend.

Sacrifice. Turn. Give. Mend.

Don't travel my journey or anyone else's. Travel yours. Bring change within this generation as you are changed again and again into the person my generation needs you to be. Allow God to continue restoring you as you are used to restore this broken generation.

Finale

From Ash to Color

My captain throws the ball and I run to catch it.

Straining with all of my being to corral it, I dive, and the wind catches me. Like a kite, I'm lifted off. Across seas and around planets, I fly and float. A shooting star races by me, showering light across my face, and just as I touch the golden dust behind it, I begin a quick and calm descent, down toward the ashen world. I set my feet down, and the building of mirrors and glass towers above me. High. Intimidating. Impenetrable.

Something happens.

The gray desert begins to shake loudly and violently in a grand seizure, rattling every bone, vein, and cell in my body. I lose myself and stumble forward. Now upon my knees, I glance up and see the building of mirrors and glass as it shivers and trembles, flexing like an accordion. It is not as impenetrable as it appears, as impenetrable as I thought. With a loud whine, and in a single deafening burst, the mirrors and glass crack and shatter. As the shards plummet to the floor, I

213

cover my head. They thump harmlessly and disappear into the ashen floor. All is still for a moment . . . but only a moment. I hear another noise now, one roaring like a thousand chariots over the horizon.

Something happens.

Previously nonexistent volcanoes emerge and erupt, spraying apple-red lava into the air. It splatters and sprinkles on the gray desert floor, instantly awakening flowers of yellow and purple. They bloom, and as they reach for the sky, the aroma of pollen fills the air and dances over the land. Beneath its airborne trail, puddles spring up in droves and then join hands to form a blue river, the purest my eyes have ever seen. Stretching and bending, and everywhere it passes, emerald trees and grass shoot up, and as they do, I realize that I no longer hear the broken symphony. The strings and flutes have fallen silent, and I hear only laughter, so much laughter. And it comes from the mouth of my generation.

Looking to my sides, I see us begin to rise up—first one by one, and then by twos and threes, leaving the ground behind, as if armed with wings. By the dozens, we lift off and full color shines through our faces and ribs as if an angelic brush applied the strokes. We fly up, all of us, except for only two: my captain, and me.

My captain looks at me and takes my hand. His touch feels warm, like victory, like overcoming, like dreams, and that warmth sprints through my body, filling every corner of me from hair follicle to toe. He lifts his eyes high, squeezes me, and we float up, joining the others, and as one, we all hover above the formerly gray, now full-color world.

Reaching slowly into his pocket, my captain withdraws a worn, rustic harmonica made of wood. He wets his lips, raises it to his mouth, and smiles a legendary smile. He taps *his feet and with the fullest joy, begins playing a melody of change and hope. Passionately and flawlessly he plays—as if he's played this song many times before. I believe he has.*

Now we all join in the rhythmic grassroots hymn, and together, we shine.

Notes

Prelude

1. Here are the cats' names: King; Glauing, also known as Kitty Sue; Aretha; Shmenry; Tiny Tim, also known as Poiky T, also known as The Man; Mr. Sautéed Mushrooms; Berman; Hannah; Bummer; Humphey—and then there are three others whose names I don't remember. (Yes, I'm fully aware of how far from normal some of the names are.)

2. I've seen people date the beginning of this generation as early as the mid-'70s, and the end of it as late as the year 2000.

3. We are also sometimes referred to as Millenials or Echo Boomers.

Death to Champions

1. The only thing better than '90s music is '80s music. It's sweet and grossly overdone, especially by the hair bands, which are my favorites. My preferred hair band is Bon Jovi, but I can't seem to garner the courage to grow a mullet, and I'm pretty sure that's the only area of my life where Kristen enables my cowardice.

True Tales of a Lonely, Lonely People

1. A few years ago, Kristen's friend Nicole lost her best friend in a car accident, and on a night of particular struggle for Nicole, Kristen came through our front door, grabbed a stack of DVDs, and drove to be with her. Before she returned, I had gone to bed, but I couldn't sleep. I just lay flat, staring at the ceiling. Late that night, I heard the front door

groan open. Assuming it was Kristen, I expected to see her walk into the bedroom moments later. She didn't, so I got out of bed to find her. A few minutes later, I discovered Kristen in the kitchen. She was leaning over the black marble counter as if she had been shot, and she had tears softly suspended in the wells of her bright blue eyes. She had refused to treat Nicole like a stranger, and paid the price for it. The pain and mess in Nicole's life got all over her, so as Nicole grieved and wept, Kristen grieved and wept with her. Love of the deep, difficult, and messy kind had brought her to tears.

The Graceless Stampede

1. *Cheers* is one of my favorite shows of the 1980s and early '90s. Some of my other favorites from that era are: *The Cosby Show*, *Saved by the Bell*, *Night Court*, *Family Ties*, *The Wonder Years*, *Boy Meets World*, *Seinfeld*, and *Magnum P.I.* (great car in that one—great mustache too).

2. Sometimes I feel like there is no rhyme or reason to the way my memory works. I'll remember a random sports statistic, but I won't remember a friend's birthday. I'll remember the smell of the food I ate in the high school cafeteria or where I was when I first heard the song "Don't Speak" by No Doubt, but I won't remember the name of someone I've met four times.

Where the Wild One Is

1. I would later sell this car for a cool $200.

2. I started getting tattoos when I was eighteen years old. My first one was very cliché: a cross with "Acts 2:25" underneath it, on my right shoulder. The guy that did the work was only a tattoo artist part time. The rest of his time he was an ultimate fighter. I've gotten a number of more tattoos since that first one, and I really like some of them. Others I have to just pretend to like. For example, I have a tattoo on my right arm that is really just a big black, well, "thing" is probably the best word to describe it. It's there for a reason though. It's covering a tattoo that I got when I was nineteen. That tattoo was meant to serve as a tribute to a girl that I was dating at the time. I didn't want to get her name on my arm; so instead, I got a symbol representing the state where she was from. Where was she from? The state of Maryland. So I got the University of Maryland's mascot on my arm. What is the mascot? A Terrapin. A red and yellow fighting turtle holding the letter "M." We broke up not too long after that, and the following year, I got the black "thing" on my arm to cover it.

Artificial Paradise

1. Ted Beasley, John Burke, Andy Stanley, Rob Bell, Ben Grice, Micah Anderson, and Bill Orris.

2. Dan Brown, Erwin McManus, Sara Gruen, Don Miller, and William Young, to name a few.

3. Scott Leger, Andrew Lloyd Webber, Amy Ray and Emily Saliers of Indigo Girls, Josh Kauffman and Paul Duncan of Kepano Green, Ed Kowalczyk of LIVE, Chris Martin of Coldplay, Cat Stevens, Josh Groban, Gerard Way of My Chemical Romance, Brandon Flowers of The Killers, Adam Gardner of Guster, and both Shane Barnard and Shane Everett.

4. When I first wrote this section, I said that I'm free from the Artificial Paradise. That's not true. I have a greater sense of freedom, but I still hear that voice that doesn't seem to like me very much. And I still sometimes believe that voice. I still hear that voice telling me I need to be more, that I'm not good enough, and that I need to hide who I am, and sometimes I listen to what that voice tells me. I still wonder if people like me, if I have value, if I'm attractive, if I'm more attractive than him or him, if you'll find value in this book, and what that means about me if you don't. But those voices are no longer the tyrants they used to be in my life. I can disagree with them and identify them for what they are . . . lies.

That Gravelly Road/Hate/A Dark Alley/Divisions/ Brother/God's Dream

1. Others movies I love, in no particular order: *Big Fish*, *The Dark Knight*, *Good Will Hunting* (remember this line? "How do you like them apples?"), *Lars and the Real Girl*, *Miracle*, *The Karate Kid*, *Dead Poets Society*, *Fletch* (one of the most quotable movies ever and, in my opinion, Chevy Chase's best), *Tombstone* (remember this line? "I'm your huckleberry"), *The Notebook*, *Anchorman* (another of the most quotable movies ever), *The Goonies*, *The Matrix* (only the first one), *Gladiator*, all the Indiana Jones movies (except for the most recent one), *Ghostbusters*, *Back to the Future I* and *II*, *Moulin Rouge*, *Rounders*, *Ocean's 11* and *13*, *The Breakfast Club*, *Slumdog Millionaire*, most of the early Tom Cruise movies, the Lord of the Rings trilogy, *Clue*, and *Rudy*.

2. Corbett and I look very much alike. She's married to a great guy (also named Josh) and is the head of a high school drama department. They have a little boy named Syrus.

3. Quinn has lived in both Costa Rica and Ecuador. She's married to another great guy, Nelson, and is by far the best writer in our family.

Wetlands

1. My friend Micah says that a "man-crush" is a nonsexual infatuation. He says that it basically means, "I want to be that person."

2. John pastors a unique community in Austin called Gateway Community Church. It's packed with wonderful people and incredible stories of changed lives. He's also a great soccer player, from what I hear.

3. Kristen and I named our dog after the famous Chicago Bears coach, Mike Ditka. I am a huge Chicago Bears fan. If they win, it makes my week. I smile more. I laugh more. I'm fun to be around. If they lose, it ruins my week, and no one wants to be around me.

4. I still read the same Bible that my mom gave me on Christmas Day, 1989.

One Last Note

Thanks so much for reading this entire book, or most of it, or some of it, or the parts that were tolerable for you. Before you close the cover, and if it's okay with you, I'd like to leave you with two things to consider.

First, if you're the corresponding type, I'd love to hear from you. Email is fine, but so is Facebook. Phone correspondence isn't an option—not because I don't want to talk to you, but simply because I hate talking on the phone. And if you're really daring, a good old-fashioned letter, written or typed (my grandmother types her letters to me on a typewriter and I love it), would be wonderful. It can be about anything— what you're learning about, dreaming about, struggling with, doubting, processing in regards to this book, or pursuing; your favorite bands, movies, or places to travel; thoughts on God, meaningful conversations you've had, steps of faith, forgiveness stories, venting grief, or joy-laden poetry celebrating a love for Christ or someone in your life.

josh@joshriebock.com
P.O. Box 163776
Austin, TX 78716

Second and lastly, if this book meant something to you— if in reading it God shook you up, squeezed your heart, or

221

invited you into a new layer of life with him and those around you; if you were moved enough that you now have a greater appetite to see healing in my generation, enough that you want to answer the cry of the broken—then please consider sharing this book with someone else. Buy them a copy or give them this one, so that they too might be shaken up and squeezed, and join God and others in the symphony of the broken.

Josh James Riebock has been a successful youth pastor and is now a sought-after speaker at conferences, colleges, and churches across the country. He speaks both to Generation Y and to people who are involved in leading this generation. He lives with his wife, Kristen, in downtown Austin, Texas.